Oil Dorado? Guyana's Black Gold (2024 edition)

Edited by

John Mair with Andrew Beck

Revised, Updated, and Enlarged **SIXTH** Edition

Cover by

Dean Stockton

Published by Bite-Sized Books Ltd 2023

Bite-Sized Books Ltd 8th Floor, 20 St. Andrews Street,

London EC4A 3AY, UK

Registered in the UK. Company Registration

No: 9395379

ISBN: 978-1-7395253-5-4

Preface

I know Guyana well. I was born and grew up there. My father, Doodnauth Singh, SC, was a barrister and later the Attorney General from 2001 to 2008. I have very fond memories of life as a child in the capital Georgetown and on weekends visiting my grandmother on the East Coast of Demerara.

The Guyana I left in 1975 was a post-colonial country with a declining economy due to the slow erosion of the sugar industry, the then backbone of that economy. It was also the time of the Forbes Burnham dictatorship. Life was tough, and often frightening, especially if you were Indo-Guyanese.

Guyana today in 2024 is a transformed country. The fastest growing economy in the world. All thanks to the discovery of 'Black Gold'- oil offshore less than a decade ago. Today, billions of barrels of sweet crude are there under the seabed waiting to be pumped out, shipped, and sold all over the world. Guyana has, almost accidentally, gone from the El Dorado - the city of gold of Sir Walter Raleigh - to Oil Dorado - the city of black gold of ExxonMobil.

One may dispute the ethics and efficacy of pumping oil in the era of climate change and the declining use of fossil fuels. But the reality is that Guyana was very poor, but now there are at least twenty years (and more?) of riches offshore to move the whole country along the road to prosperity.

My hope is that the 'Dutch disease', where oil countries are left bereft of industry after oil has come and gone and the majority of the population does not benefit, does not become the 'Guyanese disease'. Oil Dorado should see the riches lift all people in the country through better education, infrastructure, healthcare, housing, and living standards - a model of a True and Fair society.

I welcome this 2024 edition of my fellow countryman, John Mair's book. Previous editions have been best-sellers in the land of our birth. There is plenty to read and ponder in it.

'Onwards, upwards may we ever go' as goes the national song I sang as a child in Guiana.

About the contributor

Gina Miller is a social justice campaigner who successfully challenged Boris Johnson's government for its 2019 prorogation of Parliament. She is the founder and leader of the True and Fair Party.

CONTENTS

Acknowledgements

This is the sixth edition of *Oil Dorado*. Since 2019 all editions have utilised the efforts of over 100 authors. Each edition is refreshed by at least 15 new contributions, as is this one. I thank all contributors very much for their work for which nobody receives a fee. They do it for the book, for the greater understanding of the oil boom, and for Guyana.

The work of subbing these contributions is onerous and often done close to the wire. I thank Richard Lance Keeble for his work on the previous four editions, and Andrew Beck and Roger Packer for their brilliant work on the last two.

I thank all my friends, families, and contacts on both sides of the Atlantic for their support and contributions, my parents for my Guianese heritage which awoke my interest in Oil Dorado, and my wife Susan for her eternal patience and born-again interest in the land of my birth. She is a true German-Guyanese.

I leave you, dear readers, to judge (and enjoy?) the work.

John Mair

Oxford, England

December 2023

The editors

John Mair was born in the then-British Guiana (to an'Old Guianese' mother: heritage not age) in 1950. He went to Sacred Heart RC School, in Georgetown. John won the top scholarship in the Common Entrance examination in Guiana in 1961.Then his parents emigrated to the UK. He returns regularly to Guyana. He writes there under the nom de guerre Bill Cotton/Reform. John is the proud owner of a Guyana UK High Commission Award. He attended the LSE, Sussex, and Leeds universities. John has taught journalism at the universities of Coventry, Kent, Northampton, Brunel, Edinburgh Napier, and Guyana, and at the Communication University of China. He has edited 55 hackademic volumes over the last twelve years on subjects ranging from trust in television, the health of investigative journalism, reporting the Arab Spring, to three volumes on the Leveson inquiry. His most recent books have been on Inspector Morse in Oxford, ten Oxford authors, reporting the war in Ukraine, and Boris Johnson's comedic time as UK Prime Minister. He created the Coventry Conversations which attracted 350 media movers and shakers to Coventry University. Most recently, he began the My Jericho (Myjericho.co.uk) series of talks in Oxford. 300 not out at the moment. In a previous life, he was an award-winning producer/director for the BBC, ITV and Channel 4, and a secondary school teacher.

Andrew Beck worked in UK secondary, further, and higher education for 42 years, lastly as International Partnership Manager for Coventry University's Faculty of Arts and Humanities. He is the author of best-selling and oft-cited works such as *Cultural Work* and *Communication Studies: The Essential Introduction*, as well as having served as chief examiner for public and professional examinations. Retired from full-time work, he continues to teach at and advise international universities, as well as researching and publishing on a range of media issues. Recent publications include contributions to and co-editing books on Covid-19, the Ukraine war, Boris Johnson's premiership, the British monarchy, as well as occasional features for *China Eye*.

Oil

John Agard

Gushing from earth's abundance
a dream of black gold

to eel your way through fingers
coaxing a glow out of skin

or simply playing your role
of a sizzling puddle in a pan.

A little of you, says the hymn,
will keep a lamp burning

till the break of day. Sing
hosanna sing.

Yet, the ever slick one,
you anoint a prophet's brow

as well as the wheels of war.
Oil, whose side are you on?

About the contributor

John Agard, born and educated in Georgetown, Guyana, is the author of many books for both adult and young readers. He was awarded the Casa de las Americas Poetry Prize for Man To Pan, his collection of poems inspired by the evolution of the steel pan. Twice winner of the Guyana Prize, he was BBC poet-in-residence in 1998 and received the Queen's Gold Medal for Poetry in 2012.

PRELUDE: EL DORADO TO OIL DORADO - THE MYTHS AND THE MODERN REALITY

Chapter One

Sir Walter Raleigh and El Dorado: The myth traced to source

For more than 500 years the quest for El Dorado, the mythical city of gold in South America, has persisted. Nobody has ever found it, not even the original explorer Sir Walter Raleigh. **Christopher Minster** explores the background

El Dorado, the legendary lost city of gold rumoured to be somewhere in the unexplored interior of South America, claimed many victims as thousands of Europeans braved flooded rivers, frosty highlands, endless plains, and steamy jungles in the vain search for gold.

However, the most well known of the obsessed men who searched for it must be Sir Walter Raleigh, the legendary Elizabethan courtier who made two trips to South America to search for it.

The myth itself

There is a grain of truth in the El Dorado myth. The Muisca culture of Colombia had a tradition where their king would cover himself in gold dust and dive into Lake Guatavitá. Raleigh heard the story and began searchingfor the kingdom of El Dorado, 'the Gilded One'.

Lake Guatavitá was dredged and some gold was found, but not very much, so the legend persisted. The supposed location of the lost city changed frequently as dozens of expeditions failed to find it. By 1580 or so, the lost city of gold was thought to be in the mountains of present-day Guyana, a harsh and inaccessible place. The city of gold was referred to as El Dorado or Manoa, after a city told of by a Spaniard who had been held captive by natives for ten years.

Sir Walter arrives

Sir Walter Raleigh was a member of the court of Queen Elizabeth I of England, whose favour he enjoyed. He was a true Renaissance man: he wrote history and poetry, was a decorated sailor, and dedicated explorer and settler. He fell out of favour with the Queen when he secretly married one of her maids in 1592. He was even imprisoned in the Tower of London for a time.

However, he talked his way out of the Tower and convinced the Queen to allow him to mount an expedition to the New World to conquer El Dorado before the Spanish found it. Never one to miss the chance to outdo the Spanish, the Queen agreed to send Raleigh on his quest.

The capture of Trinidad

Raleigh and his brother Sir John Gilbert rounded up investors, soldiers, ships, and supplies. On 6 February 1595, they set out from England with five smallships. His expedition was an act of open hostility against Spain, which jealously guarded its New World possessions.

They reached Trinidad where they cautiously checked out the Spanish forces. The Englishmen attacked and captured the town of San Jose. They took an important prisoner on the raid, Antonio de Berrío, a high-ranking Spaniard who had spent years searching for El Dorado himself. Berrío told Raleigh what he knew about Manoa and El Dorado, trying to discourage the Englishman from continuing his quest, but his warnings were in vain.

Raleigh left his ships anchored at Trinidad and took only 100 men to the mainland to begin his search. His plan was to go up the Orinoco River to the Caroni River and then follow it until he reached a legendary lake where he would find the city of Manoa. Raleigh had caught wind of a massive Spanish expedition to the area, so he was in a hurry to get under way.

He and his men headed up the Orinoco on a collection of rafts, ships, boats, and even a modified galley. Although they were aided by natives who knew the river, the going was very tough as they had to fight the current of the mighty Orinoco River. The men, a collection of desperate sailors and cut-throats from England, were unruly and difficult to manage.

Topiawari

Laboriously Raleigh and his men made their way upriver. They found a friendly village, ruled by an aged chieftain named Topiawari. As he had been doing since arriving on the continent, Raleigh made friends by announcing that he was an enemy of the Spanish, who were widely detested by the natives. Topiawari told Raleigh of a rich culture living in the mountains. Raleigh easily convinced himself that the culture was an offshoot of the rich Inca culture of Peru and that it must be the fabled city of Manoa. The Spanishset out up the Caroni River, sending out scouts to look for gold and mines, all the while making friends with any natives they encountered. His scouts brought back rocks, hoping that further analysis would reveal gold ore.

Although Raleigh thought he was close, he decided to turn around. The rains were increasing, making the rivers even more treacherous, and he also feared being caught by the rumoured Spanish expedition. He felt he had enough evidence with his rock samples to drum up enthusiasm back in England fora return venture. He made an alliance with Topiawari, promising mutual aid when he returned. The English would help fight the Spanish, and the natives would help Raleigh find and conquer Manoa. As part of the deal, Raleigh left two men behind and took Topiawari's son back to England. As they were travelling downstream the return journey was much easier. The Englishmen were joyful at seeing their ships still anchored off Trinidad.

Return to England

Raleigh paused on his way back to England for a bit of privateering, attacking the island of Margarita and then the port of Cumaná, where he dropped off Berrío, who had remained a prisoner on board Raleigh's ships while he looked for Manoa. Raleigh returned to England in August 1595 and was disappointed to learn that news of his expedition had preceded him andthat it was already considered a failure.

Queen Elizabeth had little interest in the rocks he brought back. His enemies seized upon his journey as an opportunity to slander him, claiming that the rocks were either fake or worthless. Raleigh defended himself ably but was surprised to find very little enthusiasm in his home country for a return trip to Guiana.

The legacy of Raleigh's first search for El Dorado

Raleigh would get his return trip to Guiana, but not until 1617, more than 20years later. This second journey was a complete failure and led directly to Raleigh's execution back in England.

In between, Raleigh financed and supported other English expeditions to Guiana, which brought him more 'proof', but the search for El Dorado was becoming a hard sell.

In 1617, he returned to the New World on a second expedition, this time with Lawrence Kemys and his son, Watt Raleigh, to continue his quest for El Dorado. However, Raleigh, by now an old man, stayed behind in a camp on the island of Trinidad. Watt Raleigh was killed in a battle with Spaniards and Kemys subsequently committed suicide. Upon Raleigh's return to England, King James ordered him to be beheaded for disobeying orders to avoid conflict with the Spanish. He was executed in 1618.

Raleigh's greatest accomplishment may have been in creating good relations between the English and the natives of South America. Although Topiawari passed away not long after Raleigh's first voyage, the goodwill remained, and future English explorers benefitted from it.

Today, Sir Walter Raleigh is remembered for many things, including his writings and his participation in the 1596 attack on the Spanish port of Cadiz, but he will forever be associated with the vain quest for El Dorado.

Reference

Robert Silverberg (1985) *The Golden Dream: Seekers of El Dorado*, Athens: Ohio University Press.

About the contributor

Christopher Minster is a Professor at the Universidad San Francisco de Quitoin Ecuador. He is a specialist in Latin American literature and history with a PhD in Spanish from Ohio State University.

Chapter Two

From El Dorado to Oil Dorado: A brief history of oil in Guyana

Guyana has two potential hydrocarbon basins: the Guyana Basin which extends offshore the coastal plain, and the Takutu Basin, which is much smaller and lies inland, to the south of the country on the border with Brazil. How did we get to where we are today? **John Mair** looks back ... and forward

Pre-history

1916 The first well in Guyana was drilled on the onshore coastal section of the country in the Waini, North West District.

1926 A well drilled at the Bath sugar estate produced gas which was used for domestic purposes.

Offshore: Hopes and challenges

1950 Offshore exploration commenced.

1960-1970 Offshore drilling was undertaken by several companies including Conoco, Comoro, Deminex, Oxoco, Tenneco and Shell.

1975 Shell's Abary-1 well found several shows.

1980-1990 Mobil, Total, Guyana Exploration and BHP continued the exploration effort.

1982 The Karanambo-1 well in the Takutu Basin was drilled by Home Oil Inc. The commercial future of that find did not materialise.

1991-1992 Total drilled its Arapaima-1 well but received no returns.

1996 The founders of a Canadian-based company, CGX Energy

Inc began negotiations with the Government of Guyana to acquire an offshore concession to explore for oil.

2000 June Surinamese gunboats forced an oil rig which was hired by CGX, out of the Corentyne River during an exploration exercise at its Eagle-prospect.

2000 Guyana went to the United Nations International Tribunal of the Law of the Sea (ITLOS) on the Suriname issue.

2007 ITLOS awarded 33,000 square kilometres to Guyana in its international border dispute with Suriname.
2008 American oil giant ExxonMobil commenced oil exploration offshore Guyana.

2010 Takutu Oil and Gas Inc announced that it was drilling for oil in the Takutu Basin in the Rupununi.

Exxon hits oil finally in 2015

The Liza discovery was announced in May 2015. Liza-1 was the first significant oil find offshore Guyana.

The Payara discovery was announced in January 2017.

The Snoek discovery was announced in March 2017.
The Liza Deep discovery was announced in January 2017

The Turbot discovery was announced in October 2017.

The Ranger discovery was announced in January 2018.

The Pacora discovery was announced in February 2018.

The Longtail discovery was announced in June 2018.

The Hammerhead discovery was announced in Aug 2018.

The Pluma discovery was announced in December 2018.

The Tilapia discovery was announced in February 2019.

The Haimara discovery was announced in February 2019.

The Yellowtail discovery was announced in April 2019.

The Tripletail-1 discovery was announced in September 2019.

This was Exxon's 14th discovery in the Stabroek Block.

2019 Tullow Oil announced that it made an oil discovery at the Jethro-1 well in the Orinduik Block in August. That month, Tullow also announced its second discovery, this time at the Joe-1 well in the Orindiuk Block, bringing the total number of oil wells discovered in commercial quantities to sixteen.

The Mako discovery was announced in December 2019.

The Uaru discovery was announced in January 2020.

The Redtail discovery was announced in September 2020.

2020 The gross recoverable resource for the Stabroek Block is now estimated to be more than eight billion oil equivalent barrels, including Liza and other successful exploration wells on Payara, Liza deep, Snoek, Turbot, Ranger, Pacora, Longtail, Hammerhead, Pluma, Tilapia, Haimara, Yellowtail, Tripletail and Mako.

The Uaru-2 discovery was announced in April 2021.

The Longtail-3 discovery was announced in June 2021.

The Whiptail-1 discovery was announced in July 2021

The Whiptail-2 discovery was also announced in July 2021.

The Pinktail- discovery was announced in September 2021.

The Turbot-2 discovery was announced in September 2021.

The Cataback-1 discovery was announced in October 2021.

The Lau Lau-1 discovery was announced in January 2022.

The Fangtooth-1 discovery was announced in January 2022.

The Barreleye-1 discovery was announced in April 2022.

The Patwa-1 discovery was announced in April 2022.

The Lukanani-1 discovery was announced in April 2022.

The Seabob-1 discovery was announced in July 2022.

The Kiru-Kiru-1 discovery also announced in July 2022.

The Sailfin-1 discovery was announced in October 2022..

The Yarrow-1 discovery was also announced in October 2022.

2022 The integrated oil company (Exxonmobil/CNOOC/Hess) has now made over 35 oil discoveries in the 6.6-million-acre offshore Stabroek Block. Estimated oil there eleven billion barrels.

2023 Payara is the second discovery for 2023 after the Fangtooth SE-1 well. announced towards the end of April 202.

2023 ExxonMobil is also progressing with plans for the **Gas to Energy Project** in cooperation with the Government of Guyana. Start-up is expected by the end of 2024.

The FPSOs (Floating Production, Storage and Offloading vehicles)

Current FPSOs

These are mini oil refineries. The oil is moved undersea from several wells, refined, pumped into tankers and then sent to markets worldwide.

The Liza Phase 1 development is approximately 190 kilometres offshore in water depths of 1,5001,900 metres. The project includes an FPSO vessel, **Liza Destiny**, which is currently producing more than 120,000 barrels of oil per day, from 17 wells. It has a storage capacity of up to 1.6m barrels and is offloaded every 5-10 days. It cost in development US$3.6bn.

The Liza Phase 2 development involves a second floating, production, storage and offloading vessel (FPSO), **Liza Unity**. Production on Liza Phase 2 began on 11 February 2022 and produces up to 220,000 barrels of oil per day from 30 wells, including 15 oil-producing wells, nine water-injection wells, and six gas-injection wells. Storage capacity is two million barrels, with offloading every four days. Estimated development cost: US$6bn.

The Payara development plan includes a third floating production, storage and offloading (FPSO) vessel, named Prosperity. The project will target 220,000 barrels of oil per day. A total of 41 wells are planned, including 20 production, and 21 water and gas-injection wells. Start-up in 2023. 600 million barrels in the field in total. Storage on the FPSO will be two million barrels, offloaded every four days. Development cost: US$9bn.

Future FPSOs

The Yellowtail development involves a fourth floating production, storage and offloading (FPSO) vessel, named ONEGUYANA. The largest project to date will target 250,000 barrels per day. Production is expected to begin in 2025. There will be a total of 45-55 wells producing 925 million barrels of oil. Storage of two million barrels with offloading every four days. Development cost: US$10bn.

The **Uaru project** will have 10 drill centres with 44 production and injection wells targeting over 800 million barrels of oil resources. It is anticipated that Uaru will start production during 2026 with the capacity to pump 250,000 barrels of oil per day. Size of project is 800 million barrels of oil. FPSO would have two million barrels stored, offloaded every four days. Development cost: US$12.7bn.

The floating production platform for the **Whiptail** project should start operations in 2027 with 33-72 wells and bring the Exxon-led consortium's oil output in Guyana over 1.2 million barrels per day (bpd). Storage of two million barrels on that FPSO, offloaded every 3 to 6 days. First oil late 2027. Development cost US$12.9bn.

Exxon expects to eventually have eight FPSOs in total in the Stabroek field.

About the contributor

John Mair is the lead editor of this book.

SECTION ONE: SETTING THE GUYANA SCENE IN 2024

Big oil, big issues, big profits

John Mair

Every Man, Woman and Child in British Guiana must Become Oil-minded!

— The Daily Chronicle, British-Guiana,
Tuesday 18 November 1932

This book is a labour of love: a festschrift to my mother's land and that of her mother, her grandmothers, and great grandmothers before her for two centuries. They have historical form.

I was born in the then British Guiana to an 'old Guianese' family. I go back 'home' frequently, and have seen it develop from an impoverished state, second only to Haiti in HIPC (heavily indebted poor country) terms, brains drained (including mine) to the US, Canada, and the UK, its false rebirth as a narco-economy trans-shipping 'white gold' cocaine from Colombia to the US and Europe, the long, slow death of the sugar industry (in which I was brought up), to the new light at the end of the tunnel: a huge booming oil economy, Oil Dorado!

A very brief history of oil and Guyana

The potential for oil in Guyana was recognised by Dutch explorers in the 1700s and the first onshore exploration wells were drilled in 1916. There was little offshore oil exploration interest until the late 1960s. This was followed by a period of considerable activity in the 1970s when 22 wells were drilled. Disappointingly, no offshore commercial discoveries resulted from this activity.

However, Guyana's fortunes changed in 2015 with the Liza discovery, 120miles off the coast of Guyana in deep water of some 5,719 feet, in the Stabroek Block. Since then, history has accelerated at pace. Today, Guyana is truly the world's new oil frontier. **(See Chapter Two in this volume for more detail.)**

Guyana oil fields in October 2023

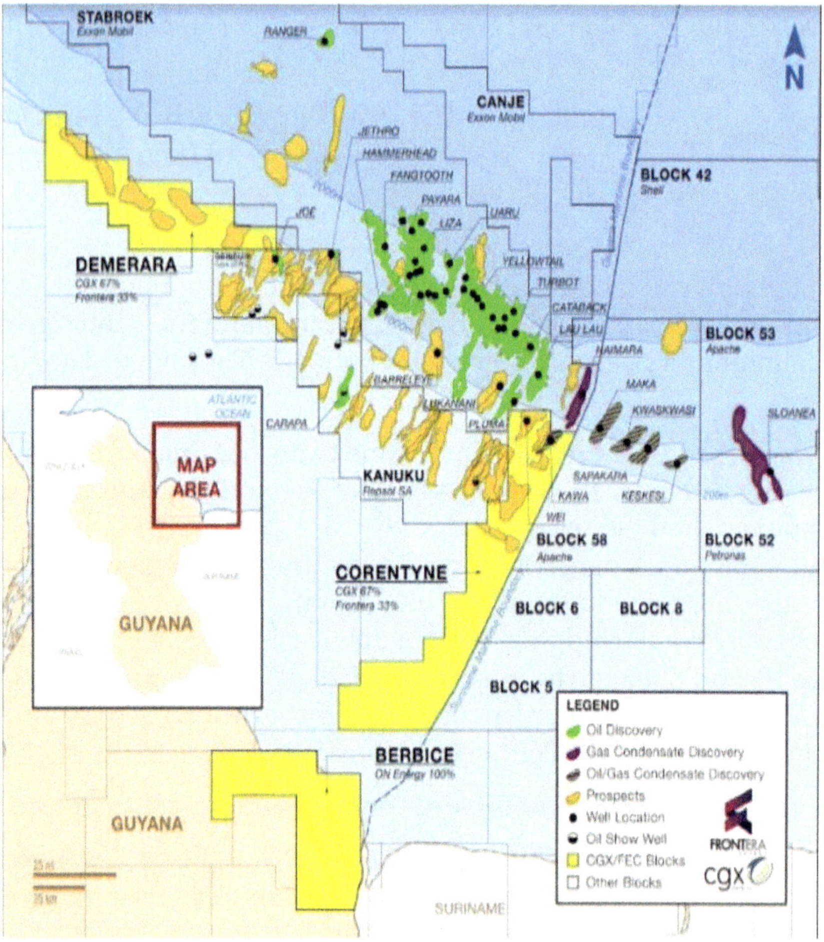

Source: CGX

Is Oil Dorado now a reality?

Five years ago, in the first edition of this book, calling Guyana 'Oil Dorado' may have verged on hype; today it is a massive understatement. Guyana is the Klondike of the oil world. Countries from India to China to Saudi Arabia and the UAE are coming calling. The multi-national oil majors from across the world - Exxon, Chevron, CNOOC for starters - are fighting to get a share of the action there or in neighbouring Suriname. In the jargon of the industry, they are 'in play' or are even 'big plays'. Oilmen talk of Guyana as the most exciting prospect, one of their most successful finds, for years.

The figures involved are quite unprecedented and simply staggering. Billions of barrels of oil are found with ease. To date, ExxonMobil and their partners have successfully drilled 35 wells in the Stabroek block alone. It may be even higher. Their hit rate of good to bad wells, wet to dry, is not far off 90 per cent, where the industry average is 20 per cent at best. Exxon estimates 11.2m barrels of oil in just that field. That is nearly a third of the world's discoveries of oil in the last five years. Guyana has gone from nowhere to number 17 in the world chart of oil reserves.

The oil just keeps flowing offshore Guyana

'First oil' was lifted in December 2019; that was just four years after it first being discovered, and a near record for Big Oil. Today, it is pumped out and refined in currently three, soon more, FPSOs (Floating Production Storage and Offloading vessels) - Liza 1, Liza Unity, and Prosperity - currently extracting 344,000 barrels of oil per day for sale on the world market. In 2023, 63 per cent of Guyana's black gold - 215000 barrels per day - went to oil-hungry Europe suffering energy shortages due to the war in Ukraine.

In essence, these FPSO vessels are floating mini oil refineries pumping oil and gas from wells nearly 6,000ft below the Atlantic Ocean. These fuels are then separated from the mud, which is pumped back in or sent ashore. At the moment so too is most of the gas. Some of that is flared. Some will be sent ashore once the pipeline to shore is set up and running in 2024. The light, sweet, high-quality (important) Brent crude is then tankered off to the world market. It is much sought after.

The Liza Phase 1, Liza Destiny is currently producing more than 120,000 barrels of oil per day, from 17 wells. It has a storage capacity of up to 1.6m barrels, offloaded every 5-10 days. It cost US$3.6 billion in development.

The Liza Phase 2 development involves a second FPSO vessel Liza Unity which produces up to 220,000 barrels of oil per day from 30 wells, including 15 oil wells, nine water injection wells and six for gas injection. Storage capacity is two million barrels, with offloading every four days. Estimated development cost is US$6 billion.

The Payara development plan includes a third FPSO vessel named Prosperity coming on stream in late 2023. The project will target 220,000 barrels of oil per day and 41 wells are planned, including 20 production and 21 water and gas injection wells. 600m barrels in the field in total. Storage on the FPSO is two million barrels, offloaded every four days Development cost is US$9 billion.

The Yellowtail development involves a FPSO vessel named OneGuyana. The largest project to date, it will target 250,000 barrels per day. Production is expected to begin in 2025 with a total of 45 to 55 wells producing 925m barrels of oil. Storage is two million barrels with offloading every four days. Development cost is US$10b.

The Uaru project, starting in 2026, will have 10 drill centres with 44 production and injection wells targeting over 800m barrels of oil resources. It is anticipated that Uaru will have the capacity to pump 250,000 barrels of oil per day. The size of the project is 800m barrels of oil with two million barrels stored and offloading every four days. Development cost is US$12.7 billion.

The floating production platform for the Whiptail project should start operations in 2027 with 33-72 wells and bring the Exxon-led consortium's oil output in Guyana over 1.2m barrels per day. The FPSO will have storage for two million barrels, offloaded every three to six days. First oil there is expected in late 2027. Development cost is US$12.9b.

Exxon expects eventually to have a total of eight FPSOs in the

Stabroek field. It is estimated that Guyana could be producing more than one million barrels per day by 2027 after the development of Yellowtail. This means that Guyana will produce more oil per capita than Kuwait!

Virtually every other month new discoveries in Stabroek block are announced. This has been one of the most prolific exploration blocks of all time. If measured on success rate, it probably does not have an equivalent in the world. In 2023 alone, ExxonMobil announced four new discoveries.

The Stabroek Field offshore Guyana: Discoveries to October 2023

Source: Rystad Energy GIS services

How much oil is there?

The oil-rich Stabroek Block is 6.6m acres (26,800 square kilometres) in size. ExxonMobil, through its subsidiary Esso Exploration and Production Guyana Limited (EEPGL), is the operator and holds a 45 per cent interest in the block. Hess Guyana Exploration Ltd holds a 30 per cent interest (since sold in October 2023 to Chevron), and China National Offshore Oil Corporation (CNOOC) Petroleum Guyana Limited, a wholly owned subsidiary of CNOOC Limited, holds 25 per cent.

Stabroek is just one block. There are eight others offshore Guyana, of which five are currently being explored.

In January 2023, the government of Guyana invited expressions of interest in 14 new offshore blocks, 11 in shallow water, three in the deep-sea area. Wood Mackenzie estimates there could be up to 25 billion barrels in those. The Petroleum Production Sharing Agreement (PSA) contracts for these are much more favourable to Guyana as a country than the 2016 ExxonMobil one. They have to be.

The government of Guyana auctioned off those 14 blocks in October 2023 on better terms for Guyana than 2016 — a 10 per cent royalty, a better profit split and a bigger signing-on bonus. Six bidders submitted offers for eight of the blocks offshore Guyana. They were awarded to companies and consortia from all over the world.

Then there is Suriname too. Back in 2012, before 'first oil', the United States Geological Survey estimated there were 13.6 billion barrels of oil and 32 trillion cubic feet of natural gas yet to be discovered in the Guyana-Suriname Basin. That ceiling has nearly been reached already. ExxonMobil recently estimated there could be up to 20 billion barrels of oil equivalent in that Basin.

In December 2021, Americas Market Intelligence estimated that by 2035 Guyana could easily be the biggest per-capita producer of oil in the world, producing 1.4m barrels per day. In 2022, Rystad Energy said Guyana would be producing more oil offshore than the US by that date. The figures are dreamlike for a Third World country, especially a former HIPC, and in October 2023 the BBC reported that the oil bonanza has transformed the Guyanese economy. According to the International Monetary Fund (IMF), it grew by 62 per cent in 2022 and is expected to add another 37 per cent in 2023. That is the fastest growth rate anywhere in the world.

How much money?

Oil quantities are beyond belief, as are oil riches. But sadly there are not too many riches for the host country. In 2016, the then government of Guyana negotiated a very lopsided Production Sharing Agreement with ExxonMobil. The oil minister at the time, Raphael Trotman, was ill advised and simply did not accept professional opinion. Guyana now gets only 2 per cent of net royalties from their oil. Many commentators argue that this is way below the going world market rate. Costs are also front-loaded to take in those of exploration pre 'first oil'. So far, according to ExxonMobil, just that one company's total investments in Guyana amounts to $62 billion. The cake is divided up so that Guyana gets but a small slice — 50 per cent of net profits once all costs are deducted. Whether that 2016 contract can or will be renegotiated forms the basis of much legal and political argument in and out of Guyana.

How profitable is Guyana oil?

Over the next ten years, the government will receive a cumulative sum of over US$14 billion from royalties and government take from the Stabroek block. That is invested in the Natural Resources Fund. As of August 2023, it had $US1.9billion in the bank. That is regularly raided, legally, by the Government of Guyana to finance long-term projects. In 2023, this could amount to $US1billion. There is now in place a supervisory board for the NRF headed by the impeccably honest Brigadier General (retired) Joe Singh.

'First oil' from the Liza Phase 1 development flowed on 20 December 2019, which was subsequently named 'National Petroleum Day' in Guyana. The Liza FPSO vessel is designed to produce up to 120,000 barrels per day. The first one million barrels of oil were lifted and exported by tanker on 20 January 2020. The Liza Phase 2 development came on stream inmid-2022 using the Liza Unity FPSO vessel. That was designed to produce 220,000 barrels per day. And it is doing just that.

In 2016, the year following the first discovery, the world oil price (Brent) hit a low of US$25 per barrel. On 29 October 2023 the price of Brent crude oil was US$90 per barrel. Liza Phase 1, 2, and Payara development break-evens are currently priced at between US$25 and US$35 per barrel.

So, the Guyana oilfields are not just plentiful but incredibly profitable!

Oil Dorado's effect on the economy and the ordinary citizen

On 16 January 2023, the Senior Minister in the Office of the President with responsibility for Finance, Dr Ashni Singh presented the National Budget for 2023. Total government spending was GY$782billion (US$3.75 billion), up by 41 per cent on 2022. There would be no new taxes but there would be investment in infrastructure. Of government revenue, nearly 30 per cent will come from oil. Guyana's economy grew by 62 per cent in 2022, and is expected to grow by a further 37 per cent in 2023 according to the IMF. The potential for per capita economic growth is huge. It has already gone up sharply. In 2015, when US oil major Exxon made its first discovery in Guyanese waters, gross domestic product per head was $11,000 (£9,380). This year, the IMF predicts it will top $60,000 (£51,000). Trickle-down economics and the multiplier effect should mean that some of that spending will percolate down to the citizen in the street. Hopefully. That too is a subject of much contention in the country.

The latent value of Guyana oil became evident when in late October 2023 the US oil major Chevron bid $US53billion for Hess Corporation's assets that included their share of the Stabroek field. In Chevron's own words, 'The Stabroek block in Guyana is an extraordinary asset with industry-leading cash margins and low-carbon intensity that is expected to deliver production growth into the next decade'. That could mean a total asset value of just that one field of $US300billion-plus. In addition, ExxonMobil also announced in late October 2023 the 'significant' discovery — their fourth in 2023 — of a new reservoir of oil in the block that they hinted could be huge. Oil Dorado is the gift that just keeps giving.

That's the big Guyana picture. Now it's time for some detailed analysis. The first section of this edition consists entirely of active contributions to the debate. It attempts to tackle the big issues facing Oil Dorado today and, maybe, offer some solutions.

First in to bat the indomitable Dr Tulsi Dyal Singh, Berbice-born but now lost in the oil badlands of Midland, Texas. He gave up medicine for investing in and chairing a bank in the Permian Basin. Tulsi observes his mother's land from afar, although with regular visits. In Trouble in the Petroverse, he looks at future for oil in Guyana as the world/the 'petroverse' changes and concludes that the Black Gold is just that, especially after the Chevron October 2023 deal to buy Hess: 'At a quarter, the value of Hess' share of the Stabroek Block is US$13 billion. At three quarters, the value US$40 billion. At a half, the value is around US$27 billion. It is tempting then to impute a current value of the entire Stabroek block. Since Hess owns 30 per cent of the Stabroek block, a range of US$50 billion at the low end to US$150 billion at the high end can be imputed.' Black Gold indeed.

All the world's press and even serious academic journals are now beating a path to Guyana. In a September 2023 piece 'Guyana is sitting on a jackpot of liquid gold' in the *Harvard International Review,* William Mao concluded 'the road to a new Guyana is long [...] That said, no number of concerns can negate the reality that Guyana has won the oil lottery, and with it the potential to lift its people out of poverty to a world of prosperity. The promise of a golden Guyana remains.'

Like journalists and commentators, oil industry analysts are swarming like moths towards the Guyana Oil Story. Sceheiner Parker is Senior Vice President and Head of Latin America for Rystad Energy. In 'The oil future for Guyana' he says about winning that oil lottery: 'As any family that wins the lottery can attest to, an influx of money typically only exacerbates latent tensions and generally causes a lot of hell-raising. If Guyana can walk this tightrope successfully remains to be seen.'

Professor Anthony Bryan is the doyen of Caribbean oil academics at The University of the West Indies (UWI) and the University of Miami. He has written in every edition of *Oil Dorado*. In his essay 'Guyana's oil and gas boom: Is it on the right track? he is clear, 'As Guyana moves forward there are very positive signs that it is going in the right direction.

Globally, investment is slowing down in new oil provinces, but Guyana's light sweet crude is an exception to the trend. Its energy resources are attracting a lot of investment.'

Another Guyanese exile, another oil expert economist, Professor Terence Yhip writes in a title that reflects a national/regional obsession — cricket — and continues the analogy to look at the future for Guyana: 'To use the metaphor of Test cricket, the outcome depends mostly on systematic and non-random factors like the quality of the captaincy; the batting, the bowling, the wicketkeeping, the fielding, and some luck for good measure.'

China has a long-term legitimate business interest in the future of Oil Dorado. CNOOC, their national oil corporation, has had a 25 per cent stake in the prolific Stabroek Field almost from the beginning. Why? Jungi Yan and Ali Hasan Humza from the Communication University of China in Beijing examine the mutual interest of the two countries in 'Why is China interested in Guyana's oil?' And, not surprisingly, they conclude that it is good for both of them, 'China has a great demand for energy, minerals, and strong infrastructure capacity, which are complementary to the economic development of Guyana'.

Among a clutch of University of Guyana Vice Chancellors, the first in to bat is the 10th 'UG' VC, Professor Ivelaw Lloyd Griffth, the office holder from 2016-2019. In 'Oil and Intimidation in the Guyana-Venezuela Saga' he closely examines the tactics of and the history of the Guyana/Venezuela border dispute until the present day. He concludes: 'the recent intimidation efforts originate in an Intimidation Playbook that dates back to the late 1960s, evidence that the South American republic with the world's largest proven oil reserves clearly has been willing to be the neighbourhood bully'.

Yet, when I spoke to him in 2016, Professor Griffith was unwilling to accept the need to adapt the curriculum of the university to the new petro-state reality. His successor does not share his view.

The current, 11th, VC, Professor Paloma Mohamed, a

playwriter and writer by trade, accepts the current reality in 'Expectation management for Guyana: A Rapidly Evolving New Producer of Oil and Gas' The VC proclaims 'we have continually addressed the fact that a different way of dealing with Guyana was necessary and possible, not only because everything about the local and global context of this moment is vastly different and calls desperately for a different way of doing business but also because it is just to forge this future'.

Still in the world of the Caribbean academia, Dr Lorraine Sobers of the UWI is the female counterpart to Anthony Bryan — the doyenne. Her original interest in oil is scientific. In 'Let them teach maths. Numbers and the young Guyanese' Dr Sobers says the answer lies in education, especially in literacy and numeracy for young people. She says, 'National progress depends on a greater proportion of the populace having a better grasp of the hard numbers that predetermine which hopes and dreams for 'One Guyana' will come true'.

In 'Plenty oil, enough enterprise in Guyana?' Professor Leyland Lucas Dean of the UG School of management doubts whether Guyana has enough conditions to release the spirit of enterprise. His considered view 'the entrepreneurial spirit is alive and well within the Guyanese society. Unfortunately, the Emperor truly has no clothes'.

Real estate prices are going through the roof in Guyana. Oilmen demand, supply responds. Prices rise. So too the prices of spare sugar estate land like the Houston Plantation slap bang in 'Shorebase Central' on the East Bank of the Demerara river. Just 500 acres left for one family but worth a king's ramson to the Vieiras. I look in 'Plantation Houston EBD: The most valuable piece of real (sugar) estate in Guyana' at the history and the prognosis for this piece of golden land in my view: 'What happens to that last 500 acres of those former sugar cane fields is a portent for Guyana's future. Sugar is dead, oil is alive. It is unlikely that the Vieira dynasty will lose out'.

GHK Lall, a 'comebackee' from the US to Guyana, is one of the more articulate, if acerbic, public commentators in Guyana. His columns in *Kaieteur News* and elsewhere often read as though he has swallowed a dictionary. When decoded, they contain much criticism of the present government, some valid. In 'Exxon's in the money. Honestly?' He looks at the unequal ExxonMobil/Guyana deal on the Stabroek Block and states, 'Some Guyanese think that Exxon could do more for Guyana, without losing its earnings leadership in the non-governmental oil world, nor its path to more riches from the Stabroek Basin. It is better for Exxon to be seen as a partner and not as some old-line capitalist predator of the most despised sort: one that is out to gouge every penny for itself out of Guyana'.

Journalist Freddie Kissoon can be equally acerbic. But in his politics he is a bit of a shopping trolley. He has switched platform for his columns from the independent *Stabroek News* to the *Kaieteur News* — now leader of the anti-oil lobby — from which he was unceremoniously removed in 2023, to today writing daily for the pro-government and state-owned *Guyana Chronicle*. In 'The Anti Oil Lobby (AOL)' he lays into the Keep it in The Ground tendency: 'What the mulato /Creole class (MCC) is doing is using the EXXON contract as their platform to weaken the government because it is their only game in town'.

Finally in this setting-the-scene section, the company CGX. It should be the bright shining star of the oil boom in Guyana. First into the field two and more decades ago. Now it is not. The CGX star is now barely glistening. Why? In 'All that glisters is not gold: The CGX story' I examine the sad history of the company which, rather than growing in size, seems to be losing limbs regularly à la Monty Python. 2023 is crunch time for CGX with the exploration of their Wei-1 well. It's make or break. The latter looks likely. At long last there should be some revenue for the company Frontera who have taken over most of CGX's assets. I conclude: 'The future onshore is not bright. Offshore there is a little more hope'.

Guyana's oil boom brings great wealth but it also brings many problems.

Read on.

Chapter Three

Five major implications of the Chevron-Hess $53bn acquisition

Leading market analyst **Arthur Deakin** looks at the recent $53 billion takeover of Hess by Chevron which vividly illustrates the massive attraction of Guyana to the oil majors and their long-term commitment to hydrocarbons in the region

The recent merging of oil and gas companies in the US indicate that energy majors see a long-term future for specific hydrocarbons in the energy transition. Chevron's $53 billion purchase of Hess, and Exxon's $59 billion acquisition of Pioneer, are likely to be the beginning of a wider industry consolidation in which oil majors target independent producers operating in relatively stable jurisdictions with proven light crude reserves, low break-even costs, and flexible oil supply (that is, shale wells that can start producing quickly when oil prices are high). Oil majors will continue to prioritise assets that generate significant free cash flows so they can continue paying large dividends to shareholders.

High interest rates make greenfield assets hard to finance

Financing greenfield energy assets in emerging markets has become extremely challenging with the rise of interest rates. Hydrocarbon assets, which most investors are shying away from, and low-carbon technologies, some of which do not yet have proven paths to profitability, are struggling to attract investments in developing markets as the risk-return is simply unjustifiable in the current financial environment. Outright acquisitions, however, have become more appealing, and none more so than the Stabroek block in Guyana. The biggest discovery in the last decade has an estimated 11 billion barrels of recoverable oil equivalent, with potential to grow even more in the future. This is a multi-decade production play, and it signals Chevron's commitment to a long-term hydrocarbon strategy in the Americas.

For years, Hess has known they have struck the jackpot with Guyana, reflected by the upbeat mood internally at the company. They have been seeking a big payday for quite some time — deservedly so, as Guyana has been praised as the best oil find in recent times. In addition to its resource potential, the ExxonMobil-operated Stabroek Block offers highly competitive break-even costs ranging from $25 to $35 per barrel. It is located offshore, where there tends to be less community opposition, and it also operates under a favourable production-sharing agreement with attractive fiscal terms.

Chart 1: Break-even costs

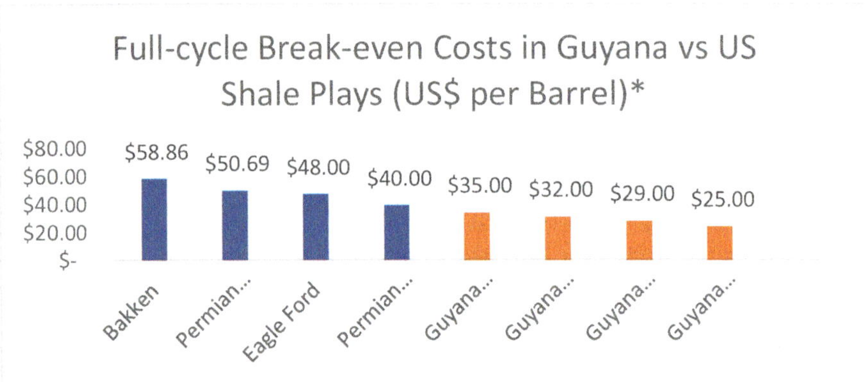

*Average full-cycle break-even prices, which is the cost of oil production, including all expenses of developing a new field such as acquisition costs and corporate-level expenses.

Source: AMI Analysis, Rystad Energy, OilNow, Mercer Capital

Five major implications for Guyana

The Chevron-Hess deal will have five major implications for the Guyanese economy, all of which are likely to lead to long-term reverberations for the local oil and gas sector:

1. **An accelerated exploration of the Stabroek block**

   Exxon's $63 billion dollars in free cash flow in 2022 makes it one of the most well-capitalised oil and gas companies in the world. The speed of their ramp-up in Guyana has been unprecedented, both in terms of time to market and successfully drilled wells. However, with another oil major joining the Stabroek consortium, it is likely that the 10 to 12 wells planned for 2024, and the 35-well exploration campaign announced through 2028, will actually exceed the original numbers.

2. **An increase in production estimates for existing wells**

   While the Stabroek consortium already has one of the most, if not the most, competent, and technical team in the oil and gas industry with ExxonMobil at the helm, there are technological advances that Chevron could bring to the table that could increase production estimates for Guyana (upwards from the 1.2 million projected for 2027). Oftentimes, these innovative technologies are siloed inside companies, with Chevron already suggesting that they will introduce new technical capabilities to the Bakken assets owned by Hess.

Chart 2: Oil production

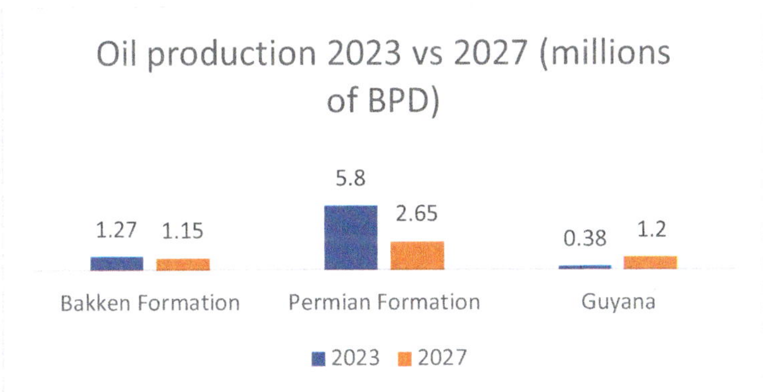

Sources: Rystad Energy, Enterprise Product Partners, AMI analysis, EIA

3. **A more competitive oil and gas sector**

   Although Exxon will still be calling the shots as the lead operator of the Stabroek consortium, the presence of another American oil major will lead to more collaborative decision-making behind closed doors. Chevron will also now be part of the bid made in the recent oil tender by Exxon, Hess and CNOOC, pacifying some of the government's claims that Exxon is the only game in town.

4. **Greater Chinese influence outside of the oil & gas sector**

   Although the third partner in the Stabroek consortium is Chinese (CNOOC), the state-owned oil company has remained in the background during the last eight years of oil development in Guyana. Now, with the presence of two of the largest American oil majors in the consortium, CNOOC's influence is likely to diminish. In turn, the Chinese government will increase its presence in surrounding sectors such as mining, healthcare, renewable power, and road infrastructure.

5. **Greater pressure from the government and the people**

   With more resources, comes greater responsibility. The Guyanese government will likely highlight this acquisition to show that interest in Guyana remains hot, using the momentum to sign production-sharing agreements that are less beneficial for oil companies in the most recent oil auction. The Guyanese people will also be more inclined to see what they can get out of a new major company coming into the country, both in terms of jobs and greater concessions. Despite the *Wall Street Journal* recently reporting that Guyana is booming, this material improvement is not being felt by the ordinary Guyanese. It is expected that there will be more public pressure for improved living conditions in Guyana.

Chevron is bullet-proofing their portfolio against international turmoil

Although Hess' 30 per cent participation in the Stabroek consortium was the main reason behind Chevron's acquisition, Hess also produces 190,000 barrels per day in the Bakken Shale Play where it owns 465,000 acres of land. The Bakken formation is both more mature and smaller than the Permian basin, signalling less room for growth, but the abundance of land means Chevron could drill new wells in new locations as old wells mature (October 2023, *Reuters*, 'Chevron-Hess deal may lift Bakken oil output, but no return to boom days'). This flexibility, during a time of geopolitical turmoil, is exactly what Chevron is looking for as it seeks to bulletproof its portfolio against unstable regimes and international conflicts.

Chevron also announced that the Bakken asset will provide a constant level of production, and strong cashflows for many years to come. In fact, if the number of rigs remain constant, at four, Chevron estimates that the Bakken acquisition will have at least 15 years of inventory (October 2023, Chevron press release, 'Chevron Announces Agreement to Acquire Hess, Edited Transcript'). Although the Bakken has high half-cycle break-even costs, at $58 per barrel, Chevron's resources means that it faces less pressure to stick to modest production increases like many other shale producers (Rystad Energy). Its deep pockets, and ability to keep providing returns to shareholders, means that Chevron can afford to take riskier bets (October 2023, *Reuters*, 'Chevron-Hess deal may lift Bakken oil output, but no return to boom days').

About the contributor

Arthur Deakin is the Director of the Energy Practice at AMI

(Americas Market Intelligence). Through market research and strategic analysis, he helps companies expand into Guyana and the wider Latin American region. In the past ten years, AMI has helped companies understand the Guyanese market, navigate Guyana's local content legislation, execute pre and post-acquisition due diligence and conduct competitive analysis on key players in the country.

Chapter Four

Wrinkles in the Petroverse

Doctor Tulsi Dyal Smith is Guyanese by birth, Texan by adoption. He heads a bank in the prolific fracking territory of the Permian Basin in Midland, Texas. He reflects on oil in his motherland

The Petroverse is showing wrinkles
crow's feet around its eyes
furrows on its forehead
and fine lines on its face
that no amount of cosmetology
can hide from revelation.

And what happens in the Petroverse
echoes exponentially in Guyana
as it learns to tame the ropes
that pull from varying directions
at the idiosyncrasies of a market
that is always unpredictable.

The landscape of Guyana's nascent petroleum industry was significantly altered in October 2023 when Chevron Corp announced its intended purchase of Hess Corporation. Earlier in the month, it was altered too, though less directly, when ExxonMobil announced its acquisition of Pioneer Natural Resources. ExxonMobil and Hess together own 75 per cent of the triumvirate which owns the mineral rights to Guyana's Stabroek block. The Chinese company CNOOC owns the other 25 per cent. ExxonMobil owns 45 per cent and is the operator of the Stabroek Block.

These ownership changes point to changes in the priorities that buyers and sellers constantly monitor and respond to in the ongoing business of enhancing shareholder value and returns, in a fast-moving and often unpredictable Petroverse.

Guyana is the sovereign owner of the Stabroek block, but the real decision-makers are the major international oil corporations that have acquired the mineral rights, have the financial resources and the technical and technological expertise to bring the oil and gas to the surface, ready for monetisation. Guyana is mostly a bystander while it receives its 2 per cent royalty and guaranteed 12.5 per cent profit share until the corporate investors have recovered their capital outlays.

John Hess, the Chief Executive Officer of Hess Corporation, was the most vocal cheerleader of Guyana's oil, as he promoted: the promises of Guyana's bountiful oil reserves; the advantaged exploitation agreement they had obtained; the pliability of their counterparts in Guyana; the ease of securing environmental passes; contracting with deepwater drillers at the bottom of a low-cost cycle; crunchy, porous rocks laden with high-quality Brent oil; and one of the lowest break-even costs in the oil industry. Hess's stock price reached its highest point ever as the corporation's profit soared. So, why did he sell, at this time, to Chevron?

Significance of the sale

The sale of Hess to Chevron involves much more than its Guyana's assets but several industry observers have cited its stake in Guyana's Stabroek Block as the crown jewel of its treasury. While the high price and the healthy premium over that price are obvious factors to motivate a sale, are there other factors that could have loaded the dice?

Financial demands of carbon capture, removal, and storage

Fossil fuels have brought incalculable benefits to mankind in the last two centuries as they powered the machinery and technologies that shape our lives today. But their production and consumption also generated petro-toxins, the most damaging of which has been carbon dioxide in the atmosphere. It is now generally accepted, even by the major oil corporations which initially denied its deleterious effect on the environment, that carbon dioxide is, in fact, a major cause of climate change; and that drastically reducing carbon dioxide in the atmosphere is an environmental, moral, and existential priority.

That daunting task will require: reductions in the production and consumption of fossil fuels; accelerated development and utilization of alternative renewable sources of energy; capture of carbon dioxide at the sources of generation; active removal from the atmosphere; and long-term storage of the captured and removed carbon dioxide underground, undersea, in seaweed farms or conversion into non-toxic or even better, into beneficial agents. This is a very expensive task and technically demanding.

In the Petroverse of the 2030s and beyond, can standalone oil producers compete with the deep-pocketed major oil companies who already have a head start and who have tight connections in Washington, DC, and have access to taxpayer dollars under the guise of research, experimentation and development through tax abatements, incentives and grants? Chevron and ExxonMobil are much closer to the biggest trough than Hess! I believe that a strategic exit now, especially at the high end of the valuation graph was a formidable reason the sale.

Recoverable reserves

The exuberant announcements of increases in the recoverable reserves in the Stabroek Block, in the billions of barrels of oil equivalent, have gone silent. The last estimate was 11b barrels of oil equivalent, and it was made more than a year and a half ago, even though eight new finds have been revealed without any change in the estimated recoverable reserves. Why? Have the new discoveries not added significantly to the cumulative total? Or, have the new discoveries only replenished the oil that is currently being extracted as rapidly as possible? Or were the initial estimates too high? Or, is there a new corporate policy to limit or delay publication of this information? Surely, both buyer and seller know the answer, but whatever is the answer, was that a factor in this sale?

The unfriendly neighbour, Venezuela

Guyana's neighbour to the west is Venezuela, the country with the largest petroleum reserves in the world. At over 300 billion barrels of recoverable reserves, it dwarfs Guyana's current 11 billion barrels. Venezuela has a very active, ongoing and ominous boundary dispute with Guyana, claiming about two-thirds of the land area of Guyana as its territory. This boundary was settled more than a century ago but has flared up intermittently by Venezuela, sometimes with belligerence. Venezuela has called a national referendum for December 2023, in Venezuela, to justify continuing its spurious claim. The result of the referendum is a foregone conclusion and will likely have the only effect of galvanising Venezuelan jingoism.

There is an open case related to the boundary, currently before the International Court of Justice. It has been dragging on for several years, largely because of non-cooperation from Venezuela, an indication of the weakness of its case. More concerning is the present build-up of troops along the border. Venezuela, with a population of over 28m people, has a vastly superior military establishment compared with Guyana which has a population of less than one million and a basic defence force. A sustained military operation would be grossly asymmetrical.

Venezuela and the major American international oil companies have had a contentious history over the last two decades. From producing a high of 3.7m barrels of oil per day, Venezuela's production is now less than one million barrels per day, largely because of its nationalisation of American oil assets and the resulting sanctions imposed on Venezuela by the United States government. The sanctions and the resulting diminution in oil revenues have devastated the Venezuelan economy to the extent that more than seven million Venezuelans have departed the country. But on October 18, 2023, the US government temporarily suspended the sanctions that applied to oil and gas operations in Venezuela. Both Chevron and ExxonMobil had huge footprints in Venezuela. Chevron still has, through a special deal with Petroleos de Venezuela SA (PDVSA), the national oil company of Venezuela. Is this temporary lifting of the sanctions a precursor of a rapprochement between the United States and Venezuela and a harbinger of Chevron increasing its activities there and ExxonMobil's return to Venezuela? Is that reason enough to have worried Hess? And possibly provide another reason to sell when the sailing's good.

Will Chevron honour the existing carbon credit contract between Hess and Guyana?

In late 2022, Guyana got verification of 33m tons of sellable Carbon Credits for its rainforest carbon sink. Hess Corporation contracted to purchase US$750m worth of it over ten years. In fact, John Hess, CEO of Hess Corp flew to Georgetown for the signing of the agreement amidst unrestrained local delight, and the first purchase, worth US$187m, was consummated. A partial payment of US$75m was to be paid to a special account in Guyana with the remainder to be paid over the following 18months. This initial lot of 12.5m tons was dubbed 'legacy credits' since they were earned retrospectively, for the years 2016 to 2020, and the price was US$15 per ton.

It was announced that Hess would continue to purchase 2.5m tons per year for 2021 to 2025 at US$20 per ton; 2.5m tons per year for the years 2026 to 2030 at US$25 per ton, making for a total transaction of US$750m.

There has not been much publicity about any further sales of Carbon Credits. But the bigger question is if Chevron will honour the remainder of the Hess Corp's commitment to buy the remainder of credits described in the purchase agreement. At his weekly press conference on October 26, 2023, Vice President Bharrat Jagdeo announced that he was aware of the question and that he asked his staff to check with Hess and was told that Chevron will honour the contract.

The future of 'fossilenes'

Despite the almost universal acceptance that fossil fuels, which I have grouped as 'fossilenes', are a potent cause of deleterious climate changes, they are still the most reliable, portable, accessible, energy-dense and cheapest available form of energy available to most of the world. The development of renewable forms of energy such as wind, solar, tidal and others have not matched the urgency that is required for them to replace fossilenes on the scale and speed required to significantly lower carbon dioxide in the atmosphere.

Just two years ago, it appeared that there was a massive effort to accelerate a rapid transition to renewable sources of energy but the war in Ukraine quickly stymied that and since then the world has fallen back to its most reliable and easily available sources, namely oil and gas. From a prediction of declining use of oil and gas over the next 30 years, some experts are projecting a gradual increase in the demand and use of fossilenes.

A world of 'fossilenes'

It appears to me that the model that the major oil companies have been targeting involves continuing to produce oil and gas while capturing as much of the carbon dioxide at emitting sources; and launch into a massive campaign to remove huge amounts of carbon dioxide already in the atmosphere. This is where huge amounts of money will be required. I see both the acquisition of Hess by Chevron and the acquisition of Pioneer by ExxonMobil as the preamble of the development of the Petroverse of the future.

Guyana's place in the Petroverse

Guyana's contribution to the world's petroleum output is expected to be around 1.2m barrels per day by 2027, or just over 1 per cent, a significant number, especially for a new producer with such a small population. Many financial analysts, in talking about the Hess/Chevron deal have described Guyana's Stabroek Block as the crown jewel of Hess' treasures. Even though Hess' share of Guyana production accounted for less than 10 per cent of Hess' revenue in 2022, the prospects from rapidly increasing production there have encouraged some analysts to give much greater weight to Guyana's contribution to the sale price of US$53bn. Ranges vary from a quarter to three quarters!

A hypothetical value of the Stabroek Block

At a quarter, the value of Hess' share of the Stabroek Block is US$13 billion. At three quarters, the value is US$40 billion. At a half, the value is around US$27 billion. It is tempting then to impute a current value of the entire Stabroek block. Since Hess owns 30 per cent of the Stabroek block, a range of US$50 billion at the low end to US$150 at the high end can be imputed. As always, this is about oil and gas. Who can predict the Petroverse?

About the contributor

Dr Tulsi Dyal Singh is a Guyanese born American. He is a Past President of the board of trustees of the Permian Basin Petroleum museum, Library and Hall of Fame. He has degrees in medicine from the University of the West Indies, a masters degree in Health Care Administration from Trinity University, Texas; and is certified as a bank director from the Southwestern Graduate School of Banking in Texas. He has lived in Midland, Texas for more than 40 years.

Chapter Five

Guess who's coming to the Guyana International Oil Table for dinner?

It used to be a rarity for Princes, Prime Ministers, and Sheiks to come to Guyana. Today it is every day. Since the country became oil boomsville, the international airport is thronged with leaders and investors wanting to come to Oil Dorado. Guyana is reaching out to them globally. The President is clocking up Airmiles. Let's examine the dinner party guests at the Oil Dorado banquet through the prism of a selection of newspaper reports. **John Mair** is your maître d'

AFRICA TODAY

Stabroek News 30 October 2023

Over 250delegates arrive on Ethiopian Airlines for AfriCaribbean forum

The first of the 250-plus delegates disembarking from the Ethiopian Airlines flight that landed yesterday at the Cheddi Jagan International Airport, Timehri. The first person to disembark was Michael Ogbalu who is the Chief Executive Officer of the Pan-African Payment and Settlement System, which facilitates trade payments in respective local currencies.

With occupancy at hotels in the capital at capacity for the historic event that promotes transatlantic trade and investment between CARICOM and Africa, the government hopes that investment and partnership opportunities here will be looked at.

THE CARIBBEAN

TRINIDAD

Stabroek News 21 October 2023

Hundreds of Trinidadians rush for Guyana oil and gas jobs

(Trinidad Express) Over a thousand Trinidadians showed up at the C3 Centre in Corinth, San Fernando, yesterday, seeking jobs in Guyana from a company operating in the oil and gas and construction sectors. They crowded the C3 compound for hours, hoping they would be able to secure employment. But a manager at Pass Tech Ltd, which hosted the event, later explained that it was a job fair and not a recruitment exercise. Pass Tech is based in San Fernando and is the parent company of Global Tech Properties, which has operations in Guyana.

THE DOMINICAN REPUBLIC

Stabroek News 2 June 2023

Setting up of Dominican Republic Embassy in Guyana hailed

The establishment by Santo Domingo of an embassy here was hailed yesterday during the visit of Dominican Republic President Luis Abinader, and the two countries are to set up a high-level working group to advance cooperation. A joint statement from a meeting yesterday between President Irfaan Ali and Abinader said that the two leaders expressed their commitment to pursue greater collaboration, particularly in the areas of energy, agriculture, tourism, trade, ICT, infrastructure and industry.

NORTH AMERICA

USA

Estabrook News 6 July 2023

US Secretary of State arrives

Secretary of State Antony J. Blinken will travel to Georgetown, Guyana on 6 July to meet with President Dr Mohamed Irfaan Ali, Foreign minister Hugh Todd, and key members of the cabinet to discuss priority bilateral issues, including food and energy security, decarbonisation, climate resilience, forests, Atlantic cooperation, regional migration, and building local capacity.

CANADA

Guyana Chronicle 20 October 2023

PM Trudeau reassures Guyana of Canada's support for its sovereignty, territorial integrity

Canada's Prime minister Justin Trudeau has affirmed the country's continued support for Guyana's sovereignty and territorial integrity. This is according to President Dr Irfaan Ali who, on Thursday held bilateral discussions with the Canadian Prime minister during the recently held Canada-CARICOM summit which took place in Ottawa, Canada. In a post via social media, Dr Ali highlighted that during these bilateral engagements, Trudeau reassured of Canada's support for Guyana's territorial integrity.

MEXICO

Stabroek News 18 October 2023

Mexico trade team on visit, visa waiver raised

Prime Minister Mark Phillips, who is performing the functions of President, met with a visiting Mexican trade delegation, led by the Mexican Ambassador to Guyana, Mauricio Vizcaíno Crespo yesterday afternoon at the Office of the Prime minister on Camp Street. During the meeting, Phillips outlined the Government's vision for Guyana, emphasising the diversification of traditional sectors on the foundation of an economy supported by the resources from oil and gas.

EUROPE

Stabroek News 8 September 2022

Guyana oil producers ramp up exports to thirsty European refiners

HOUSTON/MADRID, (Reuters) – Oil producers in Guyana are boosting exports to European buyers seeking alternatives to

Russian crude, according to vessel monitoring data. Government bans on Russian oil since the invasion of Ukraine have spurred demand for alternative crudes, and Guyanese oil fits refiners from Britain to Italy better than rival Latin American grades do. So far this year, 49 per cent of Guyana's total oil exports have headed for Europe, up from 16 per cent in 2021. Cargoes to Europe averaged 110,000 bpd from January through early September, according to Refinitiv Eikon tanker tracking data, more than the entire daily volume shipped to all destinations in 2021.

THE MIDDLE EAST

SAUDI ARABIA

***Stabroek News* 9 July 2022**

80-member Saudi delegation in Guyana today to explore investment opportunities

As Guyana continues to attract more interest from countries and companies around the world, the country will field a large delegation from the Kingdom of Saudi Arabia this weekend to advance talks and collaboration in both the public and private sectors The almost 80-member delegation, which includes high-level Government representatives such as Deputy ministers, is slated to arrive in Guyana today for the two-day visit. The increasing interest in Guyana's blooming oil and gas industry from middle Eastern States was reflected in the fact that a Saudi Arabian company, Aramco Trading Limited, was awarded a one-year contract to lift Guyana's share of oil from the Stabroek Block.

UAE

***Stabroek News* 25 Jan 2023**

Guyana talking with Qatar, UK, UAE and India on oil blocks – Reuters

Guyana is in talks with Qatar, Britain, the United Arab Emirates and India on the possibility of directly allocating offshore blocks for oil and gas exploration in parallel with a bidding round this year, President Irfaan Ali said on Monday in Trinidad.

Reuters noted that Ali visited India earlier this month, where he encouraged companies to participate in the round and engaged in talks with the government for block allocations to state companies and on possible oil supply contracts to the Asian country. India has been pressing for access to Guyana's oil and it had been suggested that New Delhi might also be interested in sewing up one of the offshore blocks.

KUWAIT

***Newsroom* 12 September 2019 (Just before 'First Oil')**

Guyana looks for link with Kuwait in oil and gas

With the appointment of a new Ambassador of Kuwait, Guyana is looking for closer collaboration in several areas, including oil and gas. "I am confident that the bilateral cooperation between our countries will be enhanced in the years ahead and that your tenure will contribute to continuing cooperation and initiate new areas of collaboration, especially in the oil and gas sector, energy, sustainable development, agriculture and education," the President (Grainger) told Ambassador Nasser Riden al-Mptairi.

ASIA

CHINA

***Stabroek News* 31 July 2023**

Guyana and China sign MoU on investment, economic cooperation

As President Irfaan Ali today wraps up his eight-day visit to the People's Republic of China, he reaffirmed Guyana's firm support for the One China principle and told Beijing that Georgetown remained committed to expanding the already robust cooperation initiatives they share. The two governments agreed 'that regular meeting […] was important for boosting bilateral cooperation and coordination on multilateral occasions' and a Memorandum of Understanding (MoU) was signed.

INDIA

Reuters 12 January 2023

India to explore buying oil from Guyana in long-term deal

NEW DELHI (Reuters) – India's oil minister and Guyana's president have discussed government-to-government cooperation in Guyana's hydrocarbon sector, the Indian government said in a statement on Thursday. India will explore buying oil from Guyana in a long-term deal and participating in the South American country's oil and gas exploration sector, the statement said.

So that's a tour d'horizon of some of the countries interested in Oil Dorado. Nowhere was this shown better than the range of companies and countries offered franchises on eight new Guyana oil blocks in October 2023.

NEW OIL BLOCK AWARDS OCTOBER 2023

***Guyana Standard* 26 October 2023**

S3 Block to SISPRO INC (**Guyana)**

S4 Block to Total Energies (**France)** EP Guyana BV, **Qatar Energy International E&P** LLC, Petronas E&P Overseas Ventures SDN BHD (**Malaysia**)

S5 Block to **International Group Investment Inc**

S7 Block to Liberty Petroleum Corporation **USA** and **Ghana-based** Cybele Energy

S8 Block to **Exxon USA/Hess USA/CNOOC China**

S10 Block to **International Group** Investment Inc

D1 Delcorp Inc Guyana, comprising Watad Energy and Communications Limited & **Arabian Drillers of Saudi Arabia**

D2 SISPRO INC (**Guyana)**

The Guyana Oil Dinner party is plainly a hot ticket in World Oil. Whether those who come to feast will leave a decent tip when they leave is yet to see.

Guyana expects.

Chapter Six

Guyana is sitting on a jackpot of liquid gold

In September 2023 **William Mao**, of the respected *Harvard International Review*, cast his critical eye on Oil Dorado

In 2015, the oil giant ExxonMobil discovered a potential total of around 11 billion barrels of oil off the coast of the small Latin American country of Guyana. The discovery promises to change Guyana forever, catapulting the country and its people to new heights of power and wealth. Oil already generates US$1b in revenues annually for the government and will produce an estimated US$7.5 billion by 2040. By these forecasts, Guyana — an impoverished, rainforest-covered country of just 800,000 people — will become the fourth- largest offshore oil producer in the world.

But there are doubts. Questions abound over whether Guyana is prepared to manage this influx of wealth. Some critics contend that Guyana lacks the legal framework and expertise to regulate the oil bonanza, and many similar developing countries — such as neighbouring Venezuela — have also struck vast oil deposits, only to be left poorer and more politically unstable than before.

This uncertainty can be segmented into three main concerns. First, can Guyana's democracy and economy survive the oil boom? Second, can Guyana survive the effect of oil money on its ethnically divided population? Third, given the coastal country's vulnerability to climate change, is it responsible to drill for more oil?

Tiny country, tremendous oil. The resource curse

Why does this curse happen? First, burgeoning resource revenues can weaken a country's economy in what economists call the Dutch disease. This phenomenon occurs because resource revenues increase the value of a country's currency, rendering foreign currencies less valuable in that country. That makes non-oil exports from the country less competitive in global markets. A foreign investor's dollar will go further to buy exports from non-oil sectors in a less wealthy, resource-poor country than in a richer, resource-rich country. Dutch disease also refers to another danger. As petro states focus their economies on exporting a single resource, labour drains into the oil industry — and away from other sectors. This concentration of labour leaves the economy vulnerable. When resources inevitably run dry or lose value, the country has few other industries to depend on. The economy crumbles.

Guyana need not look far to see this curse at play. Petroleum has long accounted for more than 75 per cent of Venezuela's total exports. When oil prices plummeted in the 1980s and in 2014, the economy was sent spiralling. By some estimates, hyperinflation reached more than 65,000 percent in 2019. Given the Venezuelan economy's dependence on oil, if the government ever used up its oil, the economy would crater.

The second reason is that oil revenues often erode good government. Many developing countries lack the legal infrastructure to oversee the management of their vast new oil funds. With little oversight, government officials can skim off the top. Funding the government through oil revenues also decreases its reliance on taxes, weakening the link between taxpayers and the government. That emboldens politicians to forego voter concerns for selfish embezzlement.

It appears Guyana's government is already struggling to avoid these two hazards that amount to the resource curse. The country is labelled a 'flawed democracy' by the Economist Intelligence Unit, only a few points above a 'hybrid regime' like El Salvador (whose leader is notoriously anti-democratic). Guyana's Corruption Perceptions Index (CPI) rating is relatively low at 41 points, lower than the global average of 43. Starting with a weak democracy and significant corruption does not bode well for the future of Guyana's governmental institutions.

Some also say the deal that the country struck with Exxon heavily favours the oil giant, guaranteeing a 50-50 split of oil revenues — lower than the average 75 per cent that most governments receive. Exxon says it took a risk working in a country with little energy infrastructure, but not everyone is convinced. The deal was signed after Exxon had confirmed the existence of the oil. It also affords Exxon an expansive lease area: 10,350 square miles, nine times larger than Exxon's average. The dubiety of this deal suggests Guyana's government may be ill-equipped to effectively manage the oil influx. The shoddy deal itself could also spell future troubles for Guyana to exploit its oil reserves. It grants Exxon tremendous control, meaning that Guyana may not capitalise enough on its natural endowment to engender the change it imagines.

Ethnic tensions

Can the country endure even as oil funds inflame Guyana's ethnic tensions? Guyanese politics are deeply divided along ethnic lines. Afro-Guyanese (descendants of African slaves) support A Partnership for National Unity (APNU), while Indo-Guyanese (descendants of Indian indentured workers) back the People's Progressive Party (PPP). In 2020, the PPP assumed power five months after a disputed general election. The PPP only won by two seats, but with control of the government, the party can dictate policy — including how oil revenues are allocated.

That consequence of this tight victory has inflamed ethnic tensions. The APNU has already begun accusing the PPP of directing oil wealth to their constituents, the Indo-Guyanese, and away from Afro-Guyanese and other ethnic groups. The party especially worries about the Natural Resource Fund, a sovereign wealth fund that holds Guyana's excess oil revenues. In a break from recent practice, the PPP did not give the APNU a seat on the board of the fund. That made the APNU furious. It worries that, left unchecked, the PPP will direct funds to Indo-Guyanese groups disproportionately. So far, there is no hard evidence of such discrimination.

Climate considerations

The third challenge is a more existential threat to Guyana: climate change. Guyana's geography leaves it extremely vulnerable to coastal flooding. Ninety per cent of Guyanese live in low-lying regions along the nation's Atlantic coast. The capital, Georgetown, lies below sea level. For decades, seawalls have kept the roaring ocean at bay. But that may soon change. Rising sea levels are increasing the frequency and severity of coastal flooding. Crops have been flood-drowned. Ocean water at times rushes over seawalls. According to some estimates, Georgetown could be submerged by 2030.

Guyana's climate vulnerability brings into question whether it is responsible for the government to promote oil drilling — a practice that accelerates climate change.

The type of oil drilling done in Guyana — deepwater offshore drilling — also risks a more immediate danger: oil spills. Such catastrophes could cause irreparable damage to the biodiversity of a country with thousands of endemic species and covered 85 per cent by rainforests. This potential biodiversity loss could also have economic consequences. Overfishing has already hurt fish and shrimp populations, and an oil spill could decimate them. That would leave many Guyanese devastated, especially Indigenous communities who depend heavily on fishing.

The dilemma is made more difficult by Guyana's storied history with climate action. In the past, Guyana's climate vulnerability made it one of the greatest pioneers for climate action. For years, the country served as a carbon sink for Norway, sequestering oil on Norway's dime so that Norway could continue to drill off its coast. Climate activists hailed the deal as a potential model for feasible climate action.

Despite these concerns, many Guyanese still seem intent on linking their future to oil. Numbers, they say, are a deciding factor. And they have a point. Over a decade, Guyana received US$150m from Norway for leaving its oil in the ground. In one year, the government made more than double that from its own oil. This insufficient compensation for climate action occurs globally.

Guyanese also consider that the concern that oil drilling will accelerate global climate change is exaggerated. In a recent environmental impact report, Guyana's Environmental Protection Agency (EPA) found that the country will remove more greenhouse gases than it emits —even accounting for the oil drilling. Although oil production will certainly only contribute to climate change, Guyana will remain carbon-negative.

Faced with these realities, Guyana's government now sees oil as, paradoxically, a central component in its climate action plan. Oil windfalls could fund the reconstruction and expansion of seawalls. They could finance farmers affected by severe flooding. And meanwhile, Guyana's rainforests would take in more CO_2 than its oil rigs spew. Liquid gold could be the key to a safer future for Guyana — even though it could also spell the country's downfall.

Reinvesting responsibly

While serious concerns surround Guyana's oil discovery, there is yet hope for the new petroleum power. Guyana's response to this challenge should centre on a fundamental principle: reinvesting portions of its oil windfalls to shore up its climate protections and to sustain and build wealth — with or without the oil.

There are two specific strategies Guyana can use to realise this goal. The first is to invest in infrastructure, including healthcare, education, roads, and, of course, climate protections. This will ensure oil funds are used to improve Guyanese quality of life directly. Guyana has already taken positive steps in this regard. The country is building 12 hospitals, multiple schools, seven hotels, two large highways, its first deepwater port, and a large gas energy plant that will double Guyana's energy output and halve power bills. Infrastructure investments like these must continue. Expanding and improving the seawalls and other climate protections would also be costly but beneficial.

The second strategy is to invest diversely through a sovereign wealth fund. This strategy has two benefits. First, the accounts of the fund are public, so Guyanese can monitor how their government is using oil money. This transparency safeguards against corruption. Second, investing diversely through a sovereign wealth fund converts excess oil windfalls into sustainable growth that is, crucially, independent of oil. If, one day, Guyana's oil reserves run dry or oil prices plummet, a diverse fund would ensure Guyana could still pay its dues. Guyana has a good guide in this endeavour. Norway — one of the few petro states that have avoided the resource curse to achieve economic prosperity — has an enormous sovereign wealth fund valued at more than US$1.3 trillion. The fund accounts for almost 20 per cent of the government budget, which finances one of the best social nets in the world. It also contains fiscal limits on how much the government can spend from the fund. That ensures the fund is maintained and Norway can spend more should its economy fall on hard times. Many accredit the fund's success to clever, diverse investing.

Guyana has already established a sovereign wealth fund — a good first step —but the fund is not without challenges. Namely, it is managed by only one of the political parties, inflaming ethnic tensions. Nevertheless, the establishment of the fund represents a positive development.

There have been other small but positive signs, too. In 2017, Guyana joined the Extractive Industries Transparency Initiative, which requires member countries to publicly disclose how their governments reward resource rights and use oil revenues. The effort suggests that Guyana is committed to clamping down on corruption — a promising sign. In May 2023, a Guyanese court ruled that Exxon must offer an 'unlimited guarantee' to cover the cost of a potential oil spill. Exxon appealed, but the ruling nonetheless represents a significant step for Guyana. It demonstrates Guyana's commitment not only to environmental protection, but also to its judiciary system. Clearly, the courts are still willing to hold giants like Exxon accountable.

Despite these encouraging indications, the road to a new Guyana is long. The persistent challenges of an oil boom still loom — the resource curse, the Dutch curse, inequitable wealth distribution, and environmental disasters. That said, no number of concerns can negate the reality that Guyana has won the oil lottery, and with it the potential to lift its people out of poverty to a world of prosperity. The promise of a golden Guyana remains. The government just has to take the necessary precautions to realize it.

This article first appeared in the *Harvard International Review* in September 2023.

About the contributor

William Mao writes for *Harvard International Review*, and *Harvard Crimson*.

Chapter Seven

The oil future for Guyana

Is the future all bright for Oil Dorado? **Schreiner Parker** is in pole position to forecast. He is head of Rystad Energy in Latin America and the Caribbean and he is optimistic

There is no doubt that the Guyana-Suriname basin is one of the hottest exploration spots in the world, but it's worth noting that exploration efforts outside of Exxon's Stabroek block have yet to yield anything near the volume of discoveries found there. The nation of Guyana would like to see that trend reversed and has proactively set up a new bid round to achieve that goal. Attracting top offshore operators is key to the ultimate success of this bidding round and preliminary reports suggest that Guyana has done just that, although maybe not to the extent it would have liked.

There were some big names missing from the 2023 bid round. Shell famously stepped away from the Stabroek block in 1999 just before the Liza-1 well was drilled and, as one of the premier deepwater operators in the world, one would think a presence there is warranted. Petrobras, for their part, could have taken some lessons from their deepwater exploration successes and applied them to the Guyana-Suriname basin, while also taking advantage of the fact that they are neighbouring countries. Chevron is another company who has the capital and technological know-how to become a player in Guyana.

None of these companies submitted bids.

Guyana asking for a better deal

As Exxon has essentially 'de-risked' the Guyanese part of the basin, new bidders are seeing contractual terms that are different to Stabroek and more favourable to the government of Guyana. The average government take is likely to be closer to 65 per cent in the new licences, which means if there are discoveries the country can expect more money flowing into government coffers in comparison with the money made on Stabroek, which is still substantial.

Ultimately, the Guyanese will want to find, produce and monetise as much oil as possible while it's still economically feasible to do so and having a lot of exploration and production operating in multiple blocks is the quickest way to get there.

Having said all that, the 2023 bid round seems to have been an overall success. The fact that big-name players, such as Total and Qatar Petroleum, showed up as well as several other smaller players speaks to the potential that oil companies see for the country. This potential, particularly in the sub-surface, was validated by the participation of the Exxon-led consortium which currently operates the Stabroek block.

How much oil and how long will it last?

The Stabroek field contains more than 11b barrels of discoveries, the vast majority of which are still waiting to enter production. The consortium say they will invest on average US$7bn each year for the next ten years to develop that block and eventually reach a peak production of almost am and a half barrels per day by 2033. It is significant that Exxon and its partners want to acquire more acreage, on top of their current exploration and development commitments, under a fiscal regime with increased government take.

Guyana's economy is already being reshaped by oil rents. Over the next ten years, the government will receive a cumulative sum of over US$14 billion from royalties and government take from the Stabroek block. That number will only increase during the 2030s as more production is brought online. If these new blocks offer anything close to the exploration prospects held in Stabroek, the government revenue-generation potential becomes exponential. Both the government and Exxon have been relatively 'good faith' actors up to this point, if that balance can be maintained while expanding both the pool of operators and the pile of money, is as of now unknown.

I have seen the oil future. Is it called Guyana?

Guyana is becoming a byword for what oil frontier exploration success will look like in the 21st century. Now that the barrels are flowing there is an influx of interest in what was before a relatively sleepy part of the globe. Even OPEC has come calling, although membership in that cartel holds almost no upside at all for Guyana. Exxon currently produces just under 400kb/d, all from the Stabroek block, but the potential production is so much greater. If all assets that have been discovered today in the Stabroek block take the final investment decision the country could produce more than am barrels a day throughout the 2030s.

OPEC realizes that the Western hemisphere is going to be where additional supply comes to market for the next decades. Brazilian offshore and the US, coupled with the quick ramp-up of Guyana, will account for over 20m barrels per day of production by 2030. OPEC in general, and the Saudis in particular, would like to have some type of leverage there, and courting Guyana was a predictable move but one that was bound to fail.

For Guyana, this issue isn't short-term oil price, as the assets producing to date all have a break-even cost of US$35/bbl or lower. Rather, the South American nation is more concerned about long-term demand. The idea for the Guyanese is to produce as much and as fast as possible to monetise the resource while there is still an implicit value for oil. Joining the cartel would have had the opposite effect, limiting production artificially in order to influence the global price. Ecuador left OPEC in 2020 for the same reason. It could not, or would not, adhere to the assigned production quota because of fiscal necessity. And the fact is Guyanese oil will be in high demand going forward due to its specific qualities.

'Privileged' barrels

When thinking about the supply mix for oil in the late 2030s and 2040s, there are certain barrels that will be 'privileged'. These are the barrels that have the necessary and sufficient conditions to be profitable in whatever future scenario the world may see as relates to price and carbon taxes. Those conditions are low break-even cost and low emissions intensity per barrel produced. Guyana is right in line with the Brazilian pre-salt oil (oil trapped below a thick layer of salt) when it comes to emissions intensity, averaging around 9 kilograms of CO_2 per barrel. That is half the global average of 18 $kgCO_2/bbl$. As economies of scale kick in and efficiencies are realized, this emissions number could even go lower. There will always be a market for this type of crude oil, at least through to the 2050s when global oil demand is still forecast to be around half of what it is today.

Very noisy neighbour

But all this current and future success has also attracted attention of another kind altogether and its transformative effects are yet to be fully understood. Guyana's neighbour Venezuela has been roused to bring up an ancient border dispute and the emigration crisis in that country is starting to bleed over into Guyana. The International Court of Justice has, for all intents and purposes, ruled this year that the claim by Venezuela is moribund and confirmed the territorial integrity of Guyana. The issue shouldn't prevent Guyana from further oil exploration west of the Essequibo River but serves to remind them that the neighbourhood is still fractious.

More interesting is how this government and subsequent governments will manage one of the world's fastest-growing economies. For a population of 800,000 this will mean significant change, which can be both good and bad. As the diaspora continues to return home, bringing new ideas but also new ways of doing things, coupled with skilled and unskilled labour flooding into Georgetown, the country will have to grapple with what it means to be Guyanese, and how to maintain unity in a bifurcated society.

As any family that wins the lottery can attest to, an influx of money typically only exacerbates latent tensions and generally causes a lot of hell raising. If Guyana can walk this tightrope successfully remains to be seen.

About the contributor

Schreiner Parker is Senior Vice President and Head of Latin America, Rystad Energy, based in Rio de Janeiro. He has 20 years' experience of oil in the region.

Chapter Eight

Guyana's oil and gas boom: Is it on the right track?

Distinguished Caribbean energy scholar **Professor Anthony Bryan** runs the ruler over prospects for Guyana. He comes out with some optimism

Guyana's oil reserves, only discovered in 2015, are vast. They are estimated at 11bn barrels of recoverable oil – one of the highest levels per capita worldwide.

The country's current daily production of 400,000 (b/d) is projected to be more than one million b/d of oil equivalent (boe) by 2027. Although Guyana only produced its first barrels of oil in December 2019, it recorded the globe's highest GDP growth rate of 2022, a remarkable 57.8 per cent. Its annual earnings from the sector could be US$10bn by 2030. However, the global media hyperbole that is accompanying the boom is boisterous and overwhelming, and raising Guyanese public expectations to an uncomfortable level. So perhaps it is time for retrospection, a reality check, and a cautionary note.

Klondike?

Dealing with this windfall is a new experience for the Guyanese government and its people. There is a race to provide the necessary legislation, to create the institutional structures, and to devise strategies to manage an oil economy.

Obviously, one danger is the onset of the dreaded ailment known variously as the 'resource curse,' the 'paradox of plenty,' or the 'Dutch Disease where destabilisation of traditional economic sectors occurs as the resource-rich country becomes overly dependent on exports of a single commodity and suffers drastic inflationary consequences.

On August 27, 2023, vice president Dr Bharrat Jagdeo was reported in the energy publication *OilNOW* as saying 'We are hell-bent on ensuring that we do not make the same mistakes that other oil-producing countries have made.'

It will be avoided by Guyana's careful fiscal management of the energy sector, including its Local Content Act, and a 'dedicated policy' towards diversification, he further stated.

Pitfalls

But most energy analysts would still agree on some cautionary notes for Guyana.

First, it is the government's responsibility to ensure that the country has all the contractual provisions in place to earn and distribute its fair share of the windfall. The population can become frustrated by the lack of any immediate tangible benefits that they may have expected from oil revenues. Managing public expectations is critical. Also, in multi-ethnic Guyana the possibility of political and ethnic strife is a constant threat if the benefits of the windfall are not distributed evenly among the various ethnic groups.

Second, although international credit agencies report that Guyana still has a low level of corruption, regulations must be developed to control that elephant in the room. Energy exploration and production has a long supply chain, and many opportunities exist for diversion of revenue and profits.

Third, the impact of the oil and gas windfall on Guyana's economy can be convulsive. Guyana may become one of the world's richest nations per capita. But attaining high-income status from natural resource wealth does not always translate into improved human development outcomes. Citizens must be shown that the wealth generated from oil and gas will be used prudently and transparently and for the people's welfare.

Full speed ahead

Now for a reality check. Guyana is not slowing down on its oil and gas exploration and production, nor should it do so. In fact, it is preparing to auction off 14 coveted oil blocks during 2023 in its first-ever government-regulated offshore licensing round. But even with the new PSA signed with Exxon which split the revenue 50-50 with a 2 per cent royalty paid to the government,

Exxon has a sweetheart deal – considering that the global average for a government's take in offshore projects is 75 per cent.

The contract also includes a strange provision that permits Exxon to immediately recover costs for exploratory work within the lease area. Exxon effectively then pays itself back for those costs out of the oil revenue that would otherwise go to the government. With an oil field lease this large (28,806 square kilometres), easy to drill, and highly productive, Guyana should have negotiated much better! Nevertheless, the country is going to realise tremendous revenue from oil and gas for a nation of around 800,000 inhabitants.

The windfall presents many challenges. Guyana can accrue more debt even with the surplus oil money. Both the International Development Bank (IDB) and the International Monetary Fund (IMF) are advising the government to save for a rainy day and to exercise caution in the way in which it goes about taking on new loans. The IMF notes that while surging oil output could help address development needs, buffer the economy, and retire expensive outstanding public debt, it also faces risks from volatile oil prices, a slowing global economy, and possible difficulties managing the resource.

Keeping it local

Guyana's political leaders have emphasised that certain services should be reserved for Guyanese procurement. The Local Content Act seeks to protect local Guyanese companies. While this is a commendable objective, just filling percentage workforce with nationals in the name of 'local content' or giving preference to local companies that may not be up to the tasks, are mistakes to be avoided. This is not about numbers, it's about investing in the long-term benefits for the country and its people.

As Guyana moves forward, there are very positive signs that it is going in the right direction. Globally, investment is slowing down in new oil provinces, but Guyana's light sweet crude is an exception to the trend. Its energy resources are attracting a lot of investment, but there are lots of investment opportunities in the non-oil sectors as well. Large investment in agriculture for the benefit of Caricom members is a major objective and regional momentum is under way. From a business perspective, the investment opportunities in Guyana are as extensive as one's imagination or skillset, once there is a Guyanese mindset that is open to foreign investment and to regional cooperation.

Saving for the future

But there are concerns as well. Despite withdrawals in 2022 and the first half of 2023, the National Resources Fund (NRF) — its Sovereign Wealth Fund — had a market value of US$1.72 billion as of June 30, 2023. It is expected to close in 2023 with about US$2.1 billion. So, while Guyana may be immune from any serious depletion of the NRF at this time, given the massive financial inflows, tapping into it to meet budget deficits, unforeseen production failures or shortfalls, substantial declines in the global prices and markets for oil, economy crippling pandemics, and serious debt incurred for rapid infrastructure development that does not produce revenue – can all impact on future drawdowns on the NRF.

When new provinces come into massive oil wealth, the resource is often controlled and dominated at an early stage by foreign companies interested in developing oil and returning profit to their shareholders. They are very rarely interested in general national economic development. So far, the international oil companies (IOCs) in Guyana, ExxonMobil and its partners, appear to be investing in sub-sectors of the economy that advance their portfolios with some benefit to the Guyanese economy. Eventually, Guyana might find the Trinidad and Tobago model – where the state chose to be an active participant and a leader in the first stage of the country's industrialisation by becoming an equity investor in most of the energy enterprises – to be a useful initiative. Guyana will have the money to do it!

Looking forward, Guyana has attributes that can make it a regional energy leader. Its forests have created environmental space for simultaneous development of its oil resources and its net carbon sink credentials.

While it may seem to be in a contradictory position as a current victim of climate change and an actor exacerbating the problem, Guyana can become a major supplier of fossil fuel that uses the money from its oil and gas resources to invest in renewable energy and facilitate its transition and that of the Caricom region to net-zero status

A version of this piece appeared in CNG Media in September 2023.

About the contributor

Anthony T Bryan, PhD, is a co-founder of the Caribbean Policy Consortium (cpccaribbean.org), Professor Emeritus at the University of Miami, and a former Director of the Institute of International Relations at UWI, St Augustine. He has been a scholar and an independent consultant on Caribbean energy.

Chapter Nine

Can Guyana win the big cricket match that is oil?

Over the last four years Guyana has shown it can generate super-high GDP growth rates, thanks to oil. But can Guyana use the oil income productively for its future development? **Dr Terence Yhip** argues there is no easy answer because so much hangs on good governance, strong economic management, and political stability

The pace of change in Guyana has been nothing short of dizzying since oil production started in late 2019. A poor backwater country in the Latin America-Caribbean region, Guyana has risen to become a high-income developing country, as declared by the World Bank in 2023. In less than four years, Guyana has largely closed the income gap with other high-income Caribbean countries, such as Bahamas, Barbados and Trinidad and Tobago. They took more than a decade to reach that status. Now, all eyes on the world stage are fixed on this small South American country of about 800,000 inhabitants, observers are wondering how long the good economic times will last and whether Guyana will succumb to the resource curse like so many oil and gas exporters.

Laying the foundations for growth and development

Oil has triggered an unprecedented economic boom, thanks to rising production and tight oil markets. In the period 2020-2022, the economy grew by an average of 40 per cent per year. The boom is mainly investment-driven by public infrastructure and by new private investments rather than by consumption. Plain and simple, Guyana has been remaking itself. In transportation, the network of roads and bridges has been expanding. Airports have seen major extensions and upgrades. Six regional hospitals are to be built, which should vastly improve medical service in a country where the population is spread thinly over 215,000 square kilometres (the size of the

UK). Four annual budgets have focused on education and housing.

But dwarfing all of these is the 300-megawatt Gas-to-Energy Project — the largest capital project in which that Guyana has ever invested. The blackouts and the high cost of electricity that have stunted economic growth and stifled development for decades should be a thing of the past. While the project is expected to generate many hundreds of jobs during the construction phase, the measure of its success would be the long-lasting jobs created and the industrialisation brought about by easy access to affordable electricity.

The Sovereign Wealth Fund

Meanwhile, the NRF (Natural Resource Fund) has grown to almost US$1.5 billion — a good *start* compared with other oil-rich countries that have been exporting oil and gas for many decades and have little saved in absolute dollars or in proportion to the tens of billions earned. The NRF currently plays a critical role in macroeconomic stabilisation by keeping a large portion of the oil money *outside* the economy so it does not add to the money supply and fuel price inflation. Guyana has chosen to not distribute the oil wealth in the form of cash transfers, a wise decision, considering that as countries get to net zero emissions, oil may go the way of the once almighty '*King Sugar*' now struggling to survive. The emphasis on capacity building, combined with saving in the NRF 'bank account 'and protecting the social safety net, makes for balanced risk management and stewardship of a scarce and finite resource.

The new production sharing agreement (PSA) for oil fields outside the Stabroek Block is a significant improvement over the 2016 ExxonMobil PSA: a 10 per cent rather than 2 per cent royalty, a cost recovery ceiling of 60 per cent rather than 75 per cent; 10 per cent corporate tax compared with nil, and equal sharing of profit oil split. All of this means that Guyana gets a return of 28.25 per cent, almost double the 14.5 per cent under the Exxon-Mobil PSA. But note, the 28.25 per cent is ma*ximum* or *potential* figure, because an oil company can find ingenious ways to lower it by maxing out its cost recovery to 60 per cent, thereby retaining more of the income. Also, the *government take* from royalty, tax and profit oil split is stuck in the 61 per cent range, well outside the 65-80 per cent achievable range observed globally.

Sufficient but enough?

On the whole, Guyana is moving on the right development path of building productive capacity. But these are not sufficient conditions for success. Guyana needs to guard against doing too much too fast. Overconfidence often leads to costly mistakes. Energy, the flagship industry, provides a good example of this outcome. The 2022 Budget included the (165megawatt) Amalia Falls Hydropower Project. At the same time, the government is inviting tenders for an oil refinery in Crab Island in Berbice county. The government has stated the oil refinery will be privately owned — another wise decision given the history of unprofitable state-owned enterprises in Guyana and across other CARICOM states.

More than temporary growth surges

The apparent rush to front-load public sector investment comes with tremendous risks. Consider energy. If the energy projects were to come on stream, there is a good chance of overcapacity in total energy: gas-to-energy (Wales, Demerara), hydro (Amalia, Essequibo) and refined oil (Crab Island, Berbice). Taxpayers could end up subsidising oil refining, on top of subsidising sugar if the industry does not return to profitability.

The trend towards electric vehicles (EVs) is no longer in doubt. Hence, it might be better for Guyana to plan for suitable roads for EVs and charging stations, invest in wind, solar and hydro, than to build an oil refinery that could be a major money-loser. Then there is always the risk that front-loading capital investments would strain the country's limited absorptive capacity (adequate infrastructure, skilled workers and management capabilities) (Yhip 2022a) and lead to project failures and cost overruns.

Don't dream too much

It would be unwise for policymakers (and the public) to get carried away with super-high GDP growth rates because it is not unusual for oil-exporting countries that have started out at low levels of GDP (Yhip 2022b). The table below gives ample examples of growth accelerations that gave way to sluggish and even negative growth performance. Take Kuwait and Equatorial Guinea as examples. After 2012, Kuwait virtually stagnated while Equatorial Guinea contracted after reaching 150 per cent growth in 1997, dwarfing Guyana's 58 per cent in 2022.

Main lessons: a growth surge, no matter how strong and extended, is a useless predictor of growth and development in the long run; and resource-dependent economies tend to stay dependent or become more dependent.

The risk of the resource curse

This brings us to the resource curse problem (sometimes called an embarrassment of riches), plus many other challenges that Guyana will face. Dutch Disease (DD) and political instability, two of the main causes of the curse, pose the greatest risks to Guyana's development. DD will torpedo any attempt at economic diversification from petroleum extraction to export manufacturing. Guyana is no stranger to deep racial divisions, often ending in violent clashes, between Indo- and Afro-Guyanese, a conflict that has held back its development since before Independence from the UK in 1966. Hence, shared growth and zero tolerance for corruption and cronyism are essential to end this endemic problem. Furthermore, political instability feeds macroeconomic economic instability by holding fiscal and monetary policy hostage to the election cycle.

Meanwhile, Guyana must deal with a chronic shortage of skilled workers and capital, so the country urgently needs an immigration policy to attract and retain talent and to lure stable foreign capital as against opportunistic and flighty private capital, in order to move the economy forward after the oil income dries up.

Economic development is a lengthy process requiring clear-headed and capable leadership for successful outcomes. The high-performing Asian countries that are often hailed as *miracles,* having caught up with the rich countries or are rapidly closing the income and technology gaps, took decades to get where they are today. It was no miracle –miracles have no natural explanation – but the 'miraculous' work of good economics, industrial policy, good politics, strong actions by leaders to change the status quo in a direction guided by a pragmatic vision, plus a liberal dose of plain '*luck*'.

Are there useful lessons for Guyana in them? Absolutely: ensure stable economic conditions, increase national saving, nurture the private sector, reward innovation, invest in physical and human capital and, not least, accumulate knowledge and know-how.

Where is Guyana going?

Guyana is starting out with minimal foreign debt, the result of debt forgiveness under the Heavily Indebted Poor Countries (HIPC) Initiative in 1996. Oil income reduces the need for foreign borrowing and Guyana's foreign borrowing capacity is much stronger today. What can possibly go wrong? Many things but ultimately all hinge on three related conditions: Firstly, good governance, secondly, strong economic management, and thirdly, political stability.

A final word. Guyana has proven to the world its capacity for growth; the bigger challenge is to prove it has the capacity for development. Can Guyana go from rags to riches and back to rags? For sure, and one has to be realistic. Growth and development *is not* a sprint but a marathon requiring those three conditions.

To use the metaphor of test cricket, the outcome depends mostly on systematic and non-random factors like the quality of the captaincy; the batting, the bowling, the wicketkeeping, the fielding, and some luck for good measure. If there are minor weaknesses in execution, the team can still salvage the innings by making a determined effort to up their game.

But if there are fundamental deficiencies in competencies and the strategy, then…it's game over.

References

Terence Yhip (2022a), 'Rapid oil spending will strain Guyana's meagre human, capital resources; lead to disastrous results – Economist warns', available at https://www.kaieteurnewsonline.com/2022/03/19/rapid-oil-spending-will-strain-guyanas-meager-human-capital-resources-lead-to-perverse-results-economist-warns/

Terence Yhip (2022b), 'Don't be fooled by rising GDP', available at https://www.kaieteurnewsonline.com/2022/04/03/dont-be-fooled-by-rising-gdp/

About the contributor

Terence Yhip holds a PhD in Economics from McGill University. He has retired from banking, after working in various countries in the area of finance including underwriting, risk modelling, credit analysis and credit risk management. After banking, he taught briefly at the University of West Indies, Mona. He is the author of two books *The Practice of Lending: A Guide to Credit Analysis and Credit Risk* and *From Rags to Riches: Is Guyana Ready for the Oil Bonanza?*

Chapter Ten

Why is China interested in Guyana's oil?

The China National Offshore Oil Corporation (CNOOC) is a big player in the offshore Guyana oil boom. CNOOC Petroleum Guyana holds 25 per cent of the prolific Stabroek Block. Is this initiative Belt and Road, belt and braces, or just a sensible early investment? **Jungi Yan** and **Ali Hasan Humza,** of the Communication University of China, discuss the issues raised by China's developing relationship with Guyana

China has been investing heavily in developing economies globally. The foundation of any strong economic relationship hinges on mutual collaboration, trustworthiness, and time-tested reliability on both sides. In what follows we will offer an in-depth investigation into the historical significance of Guyana's oil industry and China's reasons for fostering a strong economic relationship with Guyana, specifically in oil exploration and production.

The world picture

In the past decade, more than 4,360 oil and gas discoveries have been made worldwide, including 234.9bn barrels of oil equivalent. Among them, 37major oil and gas discoveries with more than 1bn barrels of oil equivalent (about 140m tons) have been made, and new discoveries have reached 86.3bn barrels of oil equivalent. This accounts for 37 per cent of all new global oil and gas discoveries. The 37 discoveries, mostly on both sides of the Atlantic Ocean and in the Persian Gulf, accounted for 90 per cent of the world's major new discoveries. Large discoveries on both sides of the Atlantic and the Persian Gulf accounted for 76 per cent of global reserves between 2010 and 2020. Seven discoveries were made on both sides of the Atlantic Ocean, while Brazil, Guyana, and the United States accounted for nearly half of the total with 16. The two biggest discoveries are the Liza field in Guyana, and the Faihaa field in Iraq.

Stabroek pays off

The Liza oil and gas field in Guyana and the Stabroek block are the focus of investments in South America by multinational companies such as ExxonMobil. The extraordinary discoveries in Guyana and neighbouring South America will rewrite the future of these developing countries.

As early as 1991, western consortiums led by ExxonMobil entered Guyana for oil exploration, but early failures made some investors withdraw. ExxonMobil persisted because the government of Guyana offered favourable risk terms.

In May 2015, ExxonMobil discovered oil more than 6,500 metres deep and 150 metres thick in the Canya Formation mudstone cretaceous sandstone in the Deepwater Liza field. It holds as much oil as the entire Gulf of Mexico. The discovery opened the door to riches and, since then other huge discoveries have been made in Guyana and the adjacent waters of Suriname.

ExxonMobil, Hess, and CNOOC hold, respectively, 45 per cent, 30 per cent, and 25 per cent interests in the Stabroek block. In 2012 CNOOC acquired Canada's Nexen, which in 2007 had acquired the interest for participating in ExxonMobil's venture exploration project in Guyana.

After ExxonMobil announced its discovery in 2015 and brought up first oil in 2019, the country rapidly became an oil upstart. Benefiting from the oil boom, the economy begun to experience unprecedented growth. After achieving 43 per cent growth in 2020 and 20 per cent growth in 2021, the GDP of the country is set to have grown by a remarkable 49 per cent in 2022 as their oil reserves and production soar. With a population of only about 800,000, Guyana is likely to overtake Kuwait as the world's largest per-capita oil producer by 2025.

CNOOC is part of Guyana's oil boom

By May 2022, UPDATE a consortium of ExxonMobil, Hess, and CNOOC had discovered more than thirty large oil and gas fields off the coast of Guyana with estimated recoverable reserves of 11bn barrels today, up from 1.5bn barrels when oil was first discovered in 2015. The IMF forecasts that the country's output will rise from 340,000 b/d (barrels per day) in 2022 to 1m b/d or more in 2027, raising it to eleventh in world rankings of countries producing more than 1m b/d.

The country's oil is high-quality, sweet, light crude oil, which is cheap to produce and can be sold at break-even prices as low as US$25 a barrel, making it extremely cost-effective. This compares favourably with world oil prices.

In December 2022, Guyana's President Ali announced a tender for offshore blocks that could provide another twenty-five billion barrels of potential crude oil reserves. It is the country's first competitive offshore block tender. The country's discoveries have been labelled the fastest-growing 'Superbasin', attracting the attention of global oil investors.

China and Guyana: a long history

Guyana is rich in natural resources but small in population. During British colonial rule, the construction of transportation, energy, and other infrastructure was stagnant, and its economic and social development lagged considerably. The country became independent in 1966, and in 1970 Guyana's parliament decided to abolish the Queen as head of state and declared itself a republic.

In June 1972, the governments of China and Guyana formally announced the establishment of diplomatic relations. Guyana was the first country in the Caribbean to establish relations with China as well as being the first among Latin American countries to do. Chinese people have made important contributions to the development of Guyana. This has been recognised by the Guyana government who announced in 2017 that 12 January would be in future designated as the Chinese Arrival Day in Guyana.

Despite the Covid pandemic, Guyana's gross domestic product expanded by 43.5 per cent in 2020, and, according to the International Monetary Fund, grew by 20 per cent in 2021 when oil reserves and production surged. Guyana's rapid economic growth is gaining momentum. The IMF expects the country's

GDP to grow by a remarkable 49 per cent in 2022 as oil reserves and production soar. Guyana is expected to pump more than 1m barrels of crude oil a day by 2028, becoming the eleventh country in the world to reach that figure.

The success of the Guyana oil project would not only revolutionise the country's economic model, but it would also set it on a path to prosperity. Since China's reform and opening up in the 1980s, the focus of China's energy demand has been to rapidly increase the scale of energy production and consumption based on the needs of rapid economic development and to establish a relatively stable energy supply system.

China has had a sizeable advantage of infrastructure capacity and the energy demand that leads to the development of advanced developed countries, and Guyana has the energy advantage but a backward level of infrastructure construction. It may be surmised that both sides can complement each other's advantages and disadvantages. Guyana will become a rising energy star in South America, and China will obtain another stable energy supply channel.

The future

China has a great demand for energy, minerals, and strong infrastructure capacity, which are complementary to the economic development of Guyana. Benefiting from China's One Belt, One Road strategy, Chinese-funded enterprises have made contributions to the country's economic and social development. Large local infrastructure facilities, such as the Cheddi Jagan airport expansion, the east coast Demerara highway reconstruction, and national broadband, have been built by Chinese-funded enterprises, creating a large number of job opportunities for Guyanese. Bosai Mining has developed into the second-largest bauxite mining company in Guyana, becoming the main economic pillar and tax source for Linden. Given the huge potential of oil and gas exploration and development in the country, CNOOC's harvest, and the good exchanges and cooperation between the two countries in the past, the sector is expected to attract more Chinese investment in the near future.

China has also been active in other areas of the economy in Guyana such as agriculture and tourism. Chinese companies have invested in agricultural projects helping to improve agricultural productivity and efficiency. The strong ties between China and Guyana have resulted in a marked increase in tourism in recent years as well. Chinese tourists travel to Guyana and contribute to its tourism industry.

Finally, the two countries have also strengthened their political and diplomatic ties. This also helps with economic aspects as both countries have worked together in multilateral forums such as the United Nations and the Caribbean Community.

Overall, in our view, the economic relationship between China and Guyana has been mutually beneficial and has helped to improve the economic well-being of both countries. It looks promising for the future as well as both countries are keen to further expand the relationship and aim to be dependable strategic partners in the oil and energy sector.

This chapter appeared in the fifth edition of *Oil Dorado* in February 2023.

About the contributors

Junqi Yan is a professor in CUC's School of Economics and management. He previously worked for PetroChina as a systems analyst.

Ali Hasan Humza works as general manager for Beijing Yixin Qinxi Psychology Ltd. He used to work for Well Manufacturing Services China (Shell & CNPC J.V) as operations manager.

Chapter Eleven

Oil and intimidation in the Guyana-Venezuela saga

Guyana has a very troublesome neighbour — Venezuela — and has had for at least 124 years. Since Guyana joined them as a petro state, the Bolivarian republic wants to up the stakes. **Professor Ivelaw Lloyd Griffith**, the former Vice-Chancellor of the University of Guyana, is your guide to warring neighbours

Source: The Counterterrorism Group [the hatched area is that claimed by Venezuela]

Venezuela's bullying actions against petro-power-in-the-making Guyana in September 2023 calls to mind the saying *plus ça change plus c'est la même chose* (the more things change, the more they remain the same). Why so, you may ask? This is because the recent intimidation efforts originate in an Intimidation Playbook that dates back to the late 1960s, evidence that the South American republic with the world's largest proven oil reserves clearly has been willing to be the neighbourhood bully. This raises several questions, four of which are addressed here. What exactly is the latest bullying attempt? What prompted this latest Playbook effort? What are some earlier Playbook pursuits? Finally, can Venezuela be made to stop the bullying?

The latest episode

Venezuela's latest bullying attempt has two aspects. One is a statement issued by the Foreign Ministry on 19 September 2023. Among other things, the statement declared: 'The Bolivarian Republic of Venezuela strongly rejects the illegal bidding round for oil blocks currently being carried out by the Government of the Cooperative Republic of Guyana since it intends to have maritime areas pending delimitation between both countries.'

Pushing the envelope of arrogance further, the communique contended that 'the Government of Guyana does not have sovereign rights over these maritime areas and consequently any action within their limits is in violation of international law, as long as they are **not** carried out through an agreement with Venezuela.' Moreover, the missive asserted that Venezuela 'reiterates that any illicit and arbitrary concession that Guyana grants, has granted or intends to grant in the areas in question is unacceptable and violates its sovereign rights, and warns that these actions do not generate any type of rights for third parties to participate in this process.'

Understandably, this Venezuelan posture evoked swift and firm repudiation by Guyana. The OAS, the United States, and CARICOM all denounced Venezuela's position.

The Venezuelan authorities went further. Two days after the communique was issued, the country's National Assembly approved a resolution to hold a 'consultative referendum' intended to 'allow the Venezuelan people to express their views on a significant territorial dispute – Venezuela's claim over the Essequibo territories.'

Interestingly, the legislative action was partly a response to the strong response by the US to the September 19 communique. Indeed, in his 23 September speech to the United Nations General Assembly, Venezuelan Foreign Minister Yvan Gil explained: 'Two days ago, Venezuela's National Assembly unanimously decided to call our people to vote in a consultative referendum to ratify the defence of our sovereign territory against the aggressions of the American empire, which wants to lead us to a war for natural resources.'

All this begs the question: why this latest action by Caracas?

What prompted the latest move?

Venezuela's latest bullying move comes in the wake of another recent step by Guyana in its journey along the corridors of petro power — the announcement of the winners of Guyana's first-ever auction of some of its oil fields, 14 blocks, ranging from about 1,000 square kilometres to 3,000 square kilometres. The inaugural oil auction closed on September 12. Eight of the 14 blocks, 11 in shallow water and three in deep water, received bids from six groups of companies.

The announcement of the outcome of the auction bid round represented another successful step along the country's petro-power journey. In September 2023, Minister Deodat Indar provided a window into the republic's trajectory — by the end of this year, production will stand at 600,000 barrels of oil per day, and by the end of 2027 it is projected to reach 1.3m barrels per day, generated from seven Floating Production Storage and Offloading (FPSO) vessels.

Venezuela recognizes this progress and projection for what they are — phenomenal and incredibly lucrative. This latest bullying episode comes out of a hefty Intimidation Playbook, and on the eve of the 124th anniversary on October 3rd of the 1899 Arbitral Award.

Earlier bullying

It's important to recall the background to this saga. Guyana referred the controversy about the validity of the 1899 Arbitral Award to the International Court of Justice (ICJ) in 2018 after several failed resolution efforts over many decades. In keeping with its rules, the ICJ needed to consider whether it had jurisdiction to hear the matter. In December 2020, the Court decided that it did, indeed, have the relevant jurisdiction, and in March 2021 Guyana was given until 8 March 2022 to submit its memorial (case brief), which it did. Venezuela was granted until 8 March 2023 to present its Counter-Memorial, and the decision on the substantive case was expected to be made by March 2024.

However, rather than work on its Counter-Memorial, in June 2022 Venezuela filed preliminary objections to the admissibility of Guyana's petition. Under ICJ rules, the trajectory of the substantive proceedings was suspended, and Guyana was then granted until October 7, 2022, to file a response to the objections, following which the Court held hearings on the matter in November 2022. Venezuela argued that since the United Kingdom was a party to the 1899 Arbitral Award, it is, therefore, an indispensable third party to the case and the Court cannot adjudicate the matter without its consent. In April 2023, the ICJ rejected Venezuela's preliminary objection, and it found that it can adjudicate upon the merits of Guyana's claims. Thus, the case trajectory was restored, with a modification. Assuming that Venezuela will remain party to the proceedings, it now has until 8 March 2024, to submit its Counter-Memorial, with a decision on the substantive case expected by March 2025.

Guyana exposed key entries in the Playbook in its submission to the Court in March 2018 when it instituted judicial proceedings. South America's sole English-speaking republic apprised the Court of some of the instances when Venezuela had taken or threatened action to discourage and prevent economic ventures it had authorized local and foreign investors to pursue in the Essequibo area. For instance, in June 1968, Venezuela placed a notice in the *Times of London* strongly objecting to and warning against any 'concessions either granted or to be granted by the Guyana Government over the territory stretching to the West of the Essequibo River'. The following month, President Raúl Leoni issued a Decree claiming Venezuela's sovereignty over the land territory west of the Essequibo River and over the adjacent territorial waters.

Fifteen years later, in June 1981, Venezuela objected to the World Bank's consideration of financing of a hydroelectric project in the Mazaruni River, a tributary of the Essequibo River, and the following year they mounted a campaign to the European Economic Community to dissuade them from participating in Guyana's economic development. In July 2000, Venezuela intervened with the People's Republic of China to object to the issuance of a forestry concession by Guyana to Jilin Industries, Ltd, a Chinese company, and in August 2013, the Venezuelan navy seized the RV Teknik Perdana research vessel while it was conducting seismic activities off Guyana's Essequibo coast for the Anadarko Petroleum Corporation. The vessel and its crew were arrested and detained in Venezuela. This resulted to the cessation of all further exploration activities in Guyana's waters by that company.

The bullying continued, with objection in April 2014 to a hydroelectric project contemplated by Guyana and Brazil and a Decree issued by President Nicolás Maduro in July 2015, which asserted sovereignty over the entire Guyanese coast between the boundary established by the 1899 Award and the mouth of the Essequibo River. The Decree also asserted exclusive jurisdiction in all the waters adjacent to that coast out to a distance beyond 200 nautical miles. As a final example of the intimidation reported to the ICJ, in February 2018, Venezuela objected to the issuance of petroleum licences to ExxonMobil in waters near the mouth of the Essequibo River, cautioning Guyana and ExxonMobil against taking any action under Guyana's license.

Besides what was reported to the ICJ on 7 January 2021 President Maduro launched a series of sabre-rattling measures against Guyana, most notably issuing Decree No. 4.415, which claimed exclusive rights in the waters and seabed extending 200 nautical miles off the Orinoco Delta. The decree created a strategic zone called the 'Territory for the Development of the Atlantic Façade' that abuts Guyana's maritime space northwest of the Essequibo River — where several oil fields are. According to the Venezuelan Commander-in-Chief, creating the zone is 'part of the battery of legal, diplomatic, political and State actions to defend our sacred rights of 200 years of the Republic'.

The intimidation measures have coexisted with Venezuela's calls for Guyana to strike a bilateral political deal over the matter as well as diplomatic overtures to other Latin American countries to sell the case about their Essequibo claim. They adopted a new tactic in the diplomatic toolbox on September 28 2023, when President Maduro used the social network X to post the following: "I ordered the Venezuelan diplomatic team to present to the Caribbean governments precise documentation demonstrating our historical rights in the dispute over the Essequibo Territory." Thus, Venezuela is extending its diplomatic campaign to Guyana's first line of defence diplomacy protection, hoping to capitalize on sympathies, especially in the Eastern Caribbean, about the possible resurrection of the Petro Caribe concessionary oil deal.

The Intimidation Playbook is open again. Its use over the years has surely stymied Guyana's economic gains, although the bullying has fallen far short of its overall aim to stymie economic development in the Essequibo, and therefore Guyana, given the territory's size and wealth generally and the country's petroleum pursuits in particular. Still, Venezuelan leaders have become so invested in their misguided 'patria' pursuits over the last six decades that one is compelled to ask: can Venezuela be made to stop the bullying?

Can Venezuela be made to stop?

The answer to this question depends on domestic and international developments and factors. On the domestic front, several political realities spawn a healthy scepticism about the intimidation ending any time soon. For one, the Venezuela 'patria' pursuit has long been a key aspect of campaigns for political power, with contestants drumming up jingoism. Keep in mind that presidential elections are scheduled to be held in 2024 to choose an office-holder for a six-year term that begins in January 2025.

Maduro is already positioning himself to retain power by hamstringing potential challengers. In June 2023, a leading candidate, María Corinamachado, was disqualified from participating because of alleged political crimes. However, use of the Essequibo as a political football is not restricted to contestation for the presidency; it happens in relation to jockeying for National Assembly positions too. Thus, it is reasonable to expect that *la zona en reclamación,* as the area is called in Venezuelan officialdom, will feature in the next set of National Assembly and local government elections due to be held in 2025.

On the international front, there are several possible influencing factors, only two of which can be addressed here. Venezuela's pursuit of membership in the BRICS group provides an opening to explore possible behaviour modification. Guyana should work the BRICS diplomatic corridors to inform current BRICS members of the nature and consistency of Venezuela's intimidation and the awkwardness of embracing a nation with such overt designs to vanquish a nation on the way to becoming a petro-powerhouse. Guyana also has the conceptual construct for such, in the form of the Defence Diplomacy Strategy — where diplomacy has been the nation's first line of defence — that it adopted shortly after winning independence from the UK in 1966.

Beyond the border issue, the energy security partnership being developed between Guyana and Brazil offers another compelling reason for Brazil to resist having the status quo altered and therefore use its considerable political and economic leverage with Venezuela to get it to reduce, if not end, the intimidation. However, this will not automatically happen; Guyana would need to be proactive in securing this.

So, in the short term, hope and happenstance are the best that could be envisaged in so far as the end of Venezuela's bullying of its smaller and weaker neighbour is concerned, unless the international influencing factors noted above come into play. Of course, behaviour modification in the longer term will depend on the decision of the ICJ, and Venezuela's reaction, if the validity of the 1899 Award is affirmed, and if the United Nations Security Council is engaged as a compliance mechanism.

A version of this article appeared earlier in *OilNOW* in October 2023.

About the contributor

Ivelaw Lloyd Griffith, a former Vice-Chancellor of the University of Guyana, is a Senior Associate with the Centre for Strategic and International Studies as well as a Fellow of the Caribbean Policy Consortium and of Global Americans. His latest book is *Challenged Sovereignty: The Impact of Drugs, Crime, Terrorism, and Cyber Threats in the Caribbean,* published by the University of Illinois Press.

Chapter Twelve

Expectation management for Guyana: A rapidly evolving new producer of oil and gas

Professor Paloma Mohamed Martin is a Change and Communications Strategist and the eleventh Vice Chancellor of The University of Guyana. She examines how expectations in Oil Dorado might be managed

In February 2018, three years after Guyana had struck first oil, I was asked to speak at the first ever GIPEX (Guyana Oil and Gas Expo). Indeed, the University of Guyana had been requested to be integrally involved in the planning, structuring, and execution of the event. I was given five minutes to speak on 'Managing Expectations' by the organisers. It was a complex topic to address in such a short time and I chose to focus on an interstice which was not popular: the expectation that the country had of investors. This chapter is largely premised on that presentation but has been extended based on the observations in the five intervening years.

Though the standard expectation and extensive literature tends to focus on how investors are to manage the expectations of the governments, people, and institutions in countries where they invest, I felt that there needed to be some clear parameters for mutuality and reciprocity in the onset for successful, sustainable, and thriving ventures. At the time it seemed a novel position to take. However, given the evolution of the extractive resources sector in Guyana, it would appear that these early insights continue to gain significance.

Guyana a pioneer

This kind of novel and nuanced work in several sections of the University of Guyana substantially informed and supported early policy which helped Guyana achieve some remarkable global firsts. For instance, Guyana was among the first countries in the world to have a Natural Resources Fund and Act set up by the time first oil was pumped in December 2019. Indeed Guyana was among the first countries in the world to create an NRF (sovereign wealth fund) before the first barrel was produced. What was fascinating about this is that there were several environmental agencies involved in drafting and enabling the first conversations. Guyana was able to learn from other countries who had waited many years after they had started producing to create their funds to deal with emerging conditions. We had the benefit of their experiences, and in many cases ready guidance and mentorship. It was among the first countries in the world to move from discovery to production in under four years (2015 to 2019) and this required a huge amount of work on the policy and regulatory side to be developed, tested, and implemented at warp speed. For example, the crude lifting policy and local content policies had to be developed by a small, dedicated crew of people in half the usual time.

Squaring the carbon credit/oil circle

In 2023, Guyana became one of the first countries in the world to receive payments for carbon credits while being responsibly engaged in wide scale extractive industries.

A critical concern of the University has and continues to be how to reconcile Guyana's nationally accepted status as an environmentally caring and responsible state (Green and Low Carbon) with its new and upcoming status as a foremost extractive oil producer in the world. This is a deeply important question which was immediately placed front and centre of all our work in public and private space.

The critical breakthrough for me came in a meeting with a top Oil executive one day in 2018 when he described his company as an 'energy company' and in this regard oil and gas was just one set of products in a menu of many which included renewables to be considered. Thereafter, we re-articulated this in the context of Guyana and in every single conference and public discussion connected to the sector we included this context. Internally, the University responded by adding not only programmes on oil and gas but several forms of energy and engineering to support them and other industries.

Thus, we created the Institute for Energy Diplomacy which would amongst other things include the Energy Think Tank, Research policy centre and focused upskilling of professionals in all areas to with energy on the pre-production side. Specialization like energy law, accounting, insurance, shipping, talent development, auditing etc., are bolted on to those interested in diversifying into the area of energy. This provides our graduates who already had degrees in these disciplines rapid modularised focused certification in areas specific to energy, management, and oversight.

The literature on frontier oil states focusing on managing expectations generally focuses inward on the people, leadership and institutions within new producing states. However, as the world changes and people become more inter-connected and able to share experiences and information globally in real time, I theorised that this would create different conditions, expectations and ultimately pressure different forms of engagement.

Who is interested in oil in Guyana?

This 360-degree perspective assumed that while investors had expectations, so too did every interest group in Guyana and that they had much more agency of articulation in these times. It could further be assumed that while some interests might be dissimilar that generally for positive sustainable engagement to occur, some synergies had to be achieved. Where these matched with objective reality then we had the best most productive fit.

Academic work on this area suggests seven inherent areas of expectation mismatches which can lead to significant impacts. These can range from dissatisfaction and frustration to widescale national upheaval and open conflict. The seven key areas of mismatch are timing (short term vs long term), resources allocation (infrastructure vs social programmes), environment vs potentially harmful impacts; capture of society and power through capture of funds vs transparent equitable inclusive governance; investors interests versus national interests, international interest's vs state interests and international expertise, resources, and networks vs local capacity.

For Guyana, these mismatched expectations are not necessarily different from any of those in other parts of the world. However, something significantly different might be emerging here.

According to Aryeetey & Asmah, 'Expectations management is one of the inescapable challenges in modern governance. Expectations can be explicit or implicit, clear, or fuzzy. They can be realistic or unrealistic; evidence based or opinionated. The literature identifies three major expectations management strategies – laissez-faire, exaggeration (or 'overselling'), and underreporting.

There therefore, seems to be a very well-defined trajectory of expectations management based on each country's and histo-cultural context. From our observations it seems clear that now, eight years after our first significant find, Guyana is currently experiencing the effects of a *laissez-faire* expectation management strategy in which, 'citizens [exercise] the right to think, say or publish whatever they wish. In a technical field, such as oil exploration, the 'popular' cum journalistic views that are associated with a laissez-faire strategy are largely inaccurate (as in the claim by the Ugandan press that oil discovery in Hoima has resulted in 'land grabbing' by top army generals). This inaccuracy is largely attributed to the weak flow of information from government to the citizens; from technocrats to politicians; and from knowledgeable civil servants (who are, by tradition 'tight-lipped') to the journalists'.

The work quoted above did not account for the often unregulated, and possibly un-regulatable effects of new media and social media channels like Facebook, Instagram and TikTok which add to the chaotic uncontextualized construction of public narratives. These narratives can now plug into international meta-narratives about companies, countries, individuals, and activities deliberately directed by interests or simply cherry picked for some attribute by citizens. To this extent expectations are now internationally inflected, guided or even directed, making an already difficult situation onerous.

Euphoria and initial un-contextual utterances

Apart from the myth of unending riches associated with oil and gas, it is to be expected that in the early days of euphoria novice officials of new oil producing countries especially those which had been prospecting for over a century without success, can utter comments about expected untold wealth without understanding or articulating the complex context and timeline information.

Additionally, if those who officially and formally are to report news on these matters are also not prepared and trained to understand this context and to provide moderate reporting then the genie gets out of the bottle with little possibility of being rebottled.

In other words, where there is a vacuum – in an absence of factual and transparent information-it is likely to be filled with something. In this situation public and private discourse will be ill informed, speculative, precipitous, and out of context. This is what can create or exacerbate expectation mismatch. This may have been in part what happened in Guyana early on in the Oil Boom.

As the first mismatch of timing ensured in which events unfolded too fast for adequate planning though valiant attempts were made by local technocrats often without any prior training or knowledge of the complex field to respond to a deluge of complex urgent requirements. Even without the constraints of time and inexperience, scant attention was paid to the communicative and informational aspects of such massive projects which have exceptional transformative possibilities for our country and our region, and which are central to managing expectations.

Lessons learned

There are therefore both painful and positive lessons to be learned from this experience moving forward. In Guyana, a situation emerged in this *laissez-faire* context, in which well-meaning media, NGO, and other groups, who are vigilant about this important moment, began to sound strident calls for due diligence, transparency, accountability and strengthening of the local institutions which will ensure that as much of the expected wealth is trapped and used for Guyana. In 2018, 60 per cent of about 3m hits per second online about Guyana included at least three of five key tropes which seem now to be firmly embedded in a meta-narrative about Guyana's energy context. These which I call the five big Cs are: **Contract**, Local **Content,** Resource **Curse, Conscience, Conflict**, and **Corruption**. This is important to note since this has the potential of impacting conversation, expectations, national and international mood as well as expectations about distributive justice in Guyana.

Possible impact of the Five Cs on the national discourse

After eight years of repetition of these tropes, the legitimate expectation of many is for transparency by all parties and public disclosure of important aspects of decision-making and management within their proper context. This, when the conversation upon technical facts and solutions is embraced and enlarged, should function to create a more robust synergy of expectations that results in better outcomes by clarifying and addressing gaps for the general good of all parties involved.

I believe a general good is achievable.

In my brief keynote in 2018 and at every opportunity since we have continually addressed the fact that a different way of dealing with Guyana was necessary and possible, not only because everything about the local and global context of this moment is vastly different and calls desperately for a different way of doing business but also because it is just to forge this future.

Managing expectations and ensuing actions synergistically, presents an opportunity for new extractive industries and others operating in Guyana to develop newmodels of engagement and to work within a new paradigm. Indeed, we have already seen efforts in some sections to begin to address this with such provisions as the Greater Guyana Initiative

(Exxon Hess and CNOOC) and the FEC-CGX Programme for Sustainable Education. Based on this, I believe that the radical shift away from the continued inward focus to a more nuanced one that works out how investors match their own expectations with those of Guyana's that we first called for is finding some fertile ground with early good results.

This kind of 'Distributive Justice' that can emerge for alignment of expectations by all is accessible and can produce a robust social contract between investors, partners, government, and civil society. This is one of the best ways to address the expectation of Guyanese for a state in which there truly is One Guyana: 'one people, one nation and one destiny'. If this can be achieved Guyana might also once again with its key investment partners provide a positive example for the world.

References

Ernest Aryeetey and Emmanuel Asmah (2011) 'Africa's new oil economies: managing expectations', in *FORESIGHT AFRICA* 22.

Julius Kiiza, Lawrence Bategeka, and Sarah Sswanyana (2011) 'Righting resource-curse wrongs in Uganda: the case of oil discovery and the management of popular expectations', Mawazo: Journal of Humanities and Social Sciences, Makere University, 10, pp183-203.

About the contributor

Professor Paloma Mohamed Martin is a full professor and well-respected international futurist scholar. She is currently the 11th Vice Chancellor and first woman to lead the University in its 60-year history. Her area of specialization is social and behavioural change and in this regard her academic pursuits have dovetailed into her work at UG as Guyana entered into a period of rapid change driven by massive discoveries of oil.. Her key endeavours related to oil and gas include conceptualising and launching the University of Guyana's Energy Think Tank and the University of Guyana's Institute for Energy Diplomacy. In 2019, she co-authored and edited the one of the first books on Guyana's oil industry *Guyana's Oil Odyssey* published by the University of Guyana Press. She has also worked closely with NGO's and the Government of Guyana in supporting the development of Guyana's Local Content Policy and the Natural Resources Fund.

Chapter Thirteen

'Let them teach maths': Numbers and the young Guyanese

Education is the bedrock of national development for Guyana, starting at the primary school level. The shortcomings of the education system have been clear for decades and it is time for the government to get serious about the numeracy and literacy of its citizenry. It is the only way there can be any meaningful local content in the energy sector, says **Dr Lorraine Sobers**

Shakuntala Devi, Indian writer and mental calculator said, "Without mathematics, there's nothing you can do. Everything around you is mathematics. Everything around you is numbers." Guyana's policymakers ought to consider this statement for their country's national development.

Much of the information about Guyana's prosperous future is conveyed using numbers: 11 billion barrels of oil reserves; 62.3 per cent growth in 2023 in real Gross Domestic Product (GDP) reported by the International Monetary Fund (IMF); 12.3 per cent non-oil GDP growth in the first half of 2023, and production capacity expected to exceed 560,000 barrels per day (bbl) when all three FPSO (Floating Production Storage and Offloading) vessels Liza Unity, Liza Destiny, and Prosperity are fully operational in 2024.

Contentious issues are communicated with the gravitas of numbers: 10 per cent royalty, up from 2 per cent, to be paid to the Guyana Government for future leases; Guyana government allocated50 per cent oil profit on the Stabroek block, calls for G$50,000 per month for 50,000 citizens to pursue or continue their education. As legions of voices join in public discourse on the anticipated windfall of petrodollars, it is fair to ask, how many Guyanese appreciate what these numbers actually mean. Do they have realistic expectations?

Local content in numbers

The Guyanese Government is attempting ensure that the petrodollar windfall results in maximum participation and benefit to citizens by establishing a Local Content Policy (LCP). However, the LCP outlines requirements to multinational oil companies that will be difficult to achieve and sustain without big improvements in the Guyanese education system.

Without an in-depth knowledge of how GDP or royalty, for instance, are calculated, it is easy for someone to reject a low number in favour of a higher number without context or reference. Poor numeracy skills will limit individual and national progress in Guyana. Without these skills, every facet of Guyana's development, even the understanding of the world of business, energy, trade, manufacturing, agriculture, etc., will be severely limited.

Many ask the question, how can the Guyanese ensure that the young will play a vital, sustaining, central role in what is emerging? The oil and gas sector rests not only on the dollars and cents reported in the news but essentially also on advanced mathematical principles that give rise to the technologies that powers the industry.

The youth of Asian countries such as China, Japan and Korea are known worldwide for impressive numeracy at an early age. It is no coincidence that these countries are also recognized as leaders in innovation, technology and manufacturing. These countries are not in the top ten per-capita oil production or forest-cover or precious metal reserves as Guyana is now, but they are geopolitically formidable. Inarguably, the national prosperity and growth of technologically advanced countries is bolstered by the level of literacy and numeracy throughout the education system.

It all STEMS from this?

The pervasive nature of mathematics was expressed succinctly by mathematician, Katherine Johnson, "We will always have

STEM (Science, Technology, Engineering and Mathematics) with us. Some things will drop out of the public eye and go away, but there will always be science, engineering, and technology. And there will always, always be mathematics."

Recent data has shown that 80 per cent of Guyanese do not have a passing grade in both Maths and English at the CSEC (Caribbean Secondary Education Certificate) level. Further, the Guyana Bureau of Statistics in 2021 revealed that more than 75 per cent of the working age population were not educated beyond upper secondary level (48.4 per cent up to primary school education). This is a weak point for Guyana. Low Maths scores will hinder progress in business, science, trade and local content in the energy sector. The low achievement in Maths at CSEC level (less than 40 per cent pass rate) may account for the problem of employment mismatch in Guyana's energy, agriculture, healthcare, and business sectors.

Functional literacy is another area of shortfall and is closely linked to problem solving, critical thinking, communication, confidence and core academic skills. The corporate world, specifically international business and the energy sector, is looking for these characteristics in employees. There is a glimmer of hope in programmes such as STEMGuyana. It has provided an excellent working example how to achieve this. At the time of writing, STEMGuyana had 42 learning pods engaging more than 800 students, 44 teachers and over 40 volunteers nationwide. STEMGuyana learners are entering and winning national and international robotics competitions and creating mobile apps at all age levels alongside a parent academy to support students at home.

The vision for STEMGuyana is to create engaged citizens who will spearhead tech start-ups, solve local and regional problems, fulfil capacity for local content in the oil sector and generate a 'spirit of cooperation for national development'. In other words, programmes like STEMGuyana support the core of national progress.

Getting back to basics

Back to the main question: How do we ensure that (Guyanese) youth play a vital, sustaining, central role in what is emerging? It may seem simple, but Guyana's education must focus on basic numeracy and literacy.

The LCP has a clearly stated intention for the 'enhancement of the University of Guyana' and the Government Technical Institute 'for adults interested in the energy sector'. But this and other training initiatives will only be successful if enough students emerging from the Guyanese secondary school system are prepared for any advanced technical programmes. Several indicators plainly show that the majority are not.

At present, relatively few enter the field of engineering, the crux of the energy sector, and fewer will be able to rise to upper management. Regional and international academic tests show that Guyana needs a higher proportion of students graduating with strong maths, reading comprehension, critical thinking and problem-solving skills. Guyana needs to aggressively pursue a vastly improved quality of education for the majority of Guyanese children in the primary and secondary school system right now. Enhancements of tertiary education institutions alone will not suffice.

Learning the problems

There are four shortcomings in the education system that must be urgently addressed: a shortage of trained teachers, urban-rural education inequality, secondary school students' performance in mathematics and science, and access to ICT (Information and Computer Technology). Increasing the number of trained teachers and improving rural education quality are the most critical. A solid foundation at the primary school level leads to improvement in performance through to secondary and tertiary education, which feeds into the availability of professionals to provide the technical goods and services required by the energy sector.

Lessons from other petro-states

Decades ago, Qatar, Saudi Arabia and Trinidad and Tobago faced the big challenge of developing their petroleum sectors by making significant changes throughout their education system. Trinidad and Tobago undertook an overhaul of its British-based education system soon after becoming an independent nation in 1962. As a result, by the late 1970s there were enough T&T nationals available to build, operate and later expand into a world-renowned downstream natural gas-based sector.

Overall, this approach has been successful in producing capable professionals and technicians to bolster expansion of upstream exploration and production activities and support services for over forty years. There were significant improvements in the quality of school facilities, teachers' training, greater access to and more options for technical and vocational training alongside academic subjects for students at all competency and income levels.

Will the sums add up for Guyana?

Guyana has the thrilling, awesome, challenge to administer the Local Content Programme for the development of Guyana's petroleum economy. Guyana has a reserve of capable professionals on hand, but many more are needed to increase the level, quality and volume of Guyanese participation in every area of economic prosperity and growth. The success of the LCP depends on the majority of Guyanese children having early access to a higher quality of earlier education which equips them for the tectonic task ahead.

Skyscrapers of the mind?

National symbols in the form of skyscrapers, fast cars and beautiful homes may or may not be everyone's dream for Guyana. However, at the very least, Guyanese youth anticipate access to affordable housing, education, healthcare and employment opportunities as petro-dollars flood into the country. Economists, policy and lawmakers will reduce wants and needs to hard numbers. These hard numbers influence political platforms' promises, discussions in boardrooms and the content of policy documents. Eventually, the numbers bounced around in the minds of elected leaders ricochet into laws and national budget allocations, having an impact on lives and livelihood everywhere.

National progress depends on a greater proportion of the populace having a better grasp of the hard numbers that predetermine which hopes and dreams for 'One Guyana' will come true.

This chapter is based on two articles published by the author in *OilNOW* in December 2021 and September 2023.

References

The Official Gazette, Local Content Act 2021 — No. 18 of 2021, December 2021.

Ministry of Education, Guyana (2021) 'Caribbean Secondary Education Certificate Examination May/June 2021 Preliminary Report on Preliminary Results'.

Ministry of Education, Guyana (2020) 'Education Sector Plan 2021-2025, Eliminating Illiteracy Enhancing Tolerance &modernizing Education'.

About the contributor

Dr Lorraine Sobers is a Fulbright Scholar and SPE Certified Engineer currently lecturing at the University of the West Indies, St. Augustine. Dr Sobers has a BS in Chemical Engineering, and postgraduate degrees, MS and PhD, in Petroleum Engineering from Texas Tech and Imperial College, London respectively. She has 20 years' experience in the energy sector specializing in Carbon Capture and Storage (CCS). Dr Sobers is a Fellow of the Caribbean Policy Consortium.

Chapter Fourteen

Plenty oil, enough enterprise in Guyana?

Can Guyanese businesses benefit in the long run from the oil boom? **Professor Leyland Lucas**, the Dean of the University of Guyana Management School asks whether the hard oil is matched by enough spirit of enterprise?

As we transform the Guyanese economy, there is common talk about the business opportunities that are available to local businesses. One only needs to open the newspapers on a daily basis and see stories of new businesses emerging and ways in which others may be able to emerge. In fact, if one examines much of the rhetoric, one may conclude that all systems are go and that opportunities abound, simply waiting to be exploited. Nonetheless, all that glitters is not gold. And, upon further examination, one may discover that in reality 'The Emperor has no clothes!'

As a people, there are numerous examples in our history about the entrepreneurial spirit that dominates our lives. African-Guyanese, having been brought forcibly from their motherlands and forced to work as slaves, still found ways to ensure that they could establish economic independence in a post-slavery era. The purchase of villages by the freed slaves and the establishment of thriving village economies stand as testament to the entrepreneurial spirit among them. Indo-Guyanese, though not constrained by the bonds of slavery, demonstrated an entrepreneurial spirit that has seen them become a huge part of the society in a post-indentureship era. Though simply highlighting these two dominant ethnic groups, the general point is that across the society in Guyana, an entrepreneurial spirit can be found.

Local content by law

With the emergence of the Oil & Gas sector, opportunities to launch new businesses do exist. The enactment of the Local Content Legislation is only one example of efforts to ensure opportunities are created and exploited. Similarly, previously enacted legislation related to the 20 per cent rule is also an effort to ensure that business opportunities made possible in the new economic sector can be exploited.

Despite the existence of these opportunities and the presence of legislation, opportunities recognised and exploited require a certain level of readiness. In the absence of preparedness, there are likely to be failures with lifelong consequences. Thus, the issue to be addressed is not one of the existence of an entrepreneurial spirit, but whether the ancillary systems are in place to support and grow such efforts. In essence, is the existing entrepreneurial ecosystem designed to support business development initiatives? To address this question, one needs to examine areas such as financing, training, incubation services, networks, and support systems.

Finding money for enterprise

Despite the transformation of the Guyanese economy, financing options remain limited. Most efforts at securing financing for entrepreneurial ventures require access to funding at fairly favourable rates and conditions. Unfortunately, within the Guyanese economy, most financing continues to come from the traditional banks. Such institutions are not geared to support new business development. Even if great business ideas exist, demands for collateral are significant and often place nascent entrepreneurs in a difficult situation of having to either say no or be prepared to jeopardise an important personal asset.

Moreover, the types of financing instruments remain traditional and place added burdens on borrowers. Opportunities for the embrace of Angel investing, venture capital, asset-based lending, bootstrapping have all been effectively used in other societies to support new venture creation. Unfortunately, within the Guyanese economy, financial regulators continue to frown on these developments which provide valuable opportunities to support new venture creation.

Homegrown finance

Other financial institutions also have a critical role to play within the ecosystem. Credit unions, which are the guardians of significant financial assets, must play their role in this entrepreneurship eco-system. Seeing themselves as enablers of economic activity, rather than guardians of savings, changes their standing in the national economy. With enlightened management and not much risk, credit unions can help to develop entrepreneurs and a new group of wealth generators.

For example, a member of the security forces about to retire may be able to use support from the associated credit union to engage in a new venture. That venture, if done right, will yield a level of economic success beyond merely waiting to collect one's pension and supplementing it with new employment.

Of equal concern is the absence of a financing institution designed to support the launch and financing of new business ventures. Currently, there exists the Small Business Bureau and GO-Invest (Guyana Office for Investment). While they continue to perform in admirable ways, the size of their budgets pales with what may be required to ensure an explosion in new businesses to match the current landscape. What is really required within the Guyanese entrepreneurial ecosystem is a major financial institution with mandate to support new business ventures. Organisations such as Go-Invest and the Small Business Bureau are necessary, but not sufficient, for entrepreneurship to grow.

No trust?

Speaking of the importance of new financial instruments to facilitate new business development, an often overlooked factor within the Guyana context is the importance of trust. Within the Guyanese economy, there is a huge trust deficit. Notions of others having the same ideas are often displaced and repeated by theft. The absence of effective enforcement mechanisms places additional pressures on the system to demonstrate that more than one person can have identical business ideas at the same time.

So long as there are stories of lapses in enforcement of laws and violations of property rights, an entrepreneurship ecosystem cannot succeed. Hence, a great deal of emphasis must be devoted to rebuilding trust for entrepreneurship to thrive.

Not just spirit but concrete too

The physical infrastructure is also important to the entrepreneurship ecosystem. Products created and ready for market require effective logistics systems, reliable power supplies, and communications networks. National resources need to be devoted to creating an exceptional road and air transportation system, a reliable power grid, and a telecommunication system that is dependable.

Products must be delivered on time to customers; delays in production due to power outages must be minimised; contacts between producers and customers must be reliable. These support mechanisms are particularly important within the context of business opportunities associated with the oil and gas sector. Entrepreneurship cannot thrive if these essential concrete support systems are not dependable.

'Homes' or incubator homes

Physical infrastructure within an entrepreneurship ecosystem may also include dedicated facilities. It is important for prospective entrepreneurs to have a place they can call 'home', a stable environment in which they can work. Hence, the need to create business incubators. While such facilities have been established in name, the reality is that the services needed for an incubator to be effective are absent from the general landscape.

Any business incubator must not only provide space for nascent entrepreneurs, but also a series of services to support their efforts to convert business ideas into scalable products and services. Doing so requires marketing services, financing options, and mentoring services. Nascent entrepreneurs must be guided through the process of moving from idea to success, with flexible guidelines on exodus from the incubator.

What do Guyanese do best?

Though there is much debate about opportunities linked to the Oil and Gas sector, an overlooked aspect of this discussion is what are Guyanese best able to provide? The reality is that we are still an agricultural and service society. Particularly from the agricultural sector, it should be recognised that opportunities for supplying produce exist. However, the ability to fully exploit these opportunities are closely linked to agglomeration economics: the willingness of farmers to unite and supply produce in the quantities needed. While a number of farmers may be interested in doing so, they are confronted with two problems: one, the trust deficit and, two, the absence of standards. The standards relate not just to product quality, but also to the manner in which business is conducted. Unfortunately, within the Guyanese economy, the rapid emergence of the Oil and Gas sector has not been matched by a level of preparation that makes the society capable of fully benefiting from these opportunities. Moreover, the lack of preparedness creates a gap filled by already established firms within the Guyanese economy, much to the chagrin of nascent players.

The spirit is alive and well. it Just needs release . . . or clothes

The essence of this chapter is that the entrepreneurial spirit is alive and well within the Guyanese society. Unfortunately, the Emperor truly has no clothes. This is reflected in the absence of training and a lack of focus on the development of the entrepreneurial ecosystem that creates limitations on the ability of that entrepreneurial spirit to emerge and thrive.

Unless there are significant investments in this area, we are unlikely to see significant benefits going to local entrepreneurs. Instead, many of these opportunities will not exploited because the tools needed to support entrepreneurs simply do not exist.

About the contributor

Dr Leyland M Lucas is the Founding Dean & Professor of Management, University of Guyana, School of Entrepreneurship & Business Innovation (SEBI). A graduate of UG, he holds several post-graduate degrees including a Doctor of Philosophy from Rutgers Business School in New Jersey USA. In a pre-academic life, he worked in the economic planning, real estate lending, banking, and non-profit sectors. Since joining academia, he has taught at several institutions in the US and in Ghana. His current research interest is Local Content, and he has served on several Advisory Boards.

Chapter Fifteen

Plantation Houston EBD: The most valuable piece of real (sugar) estate in Guyana?

It is only 500 acres of former sugar estate, yet it is maybe worth billions of US dollars to one Guyanese family. How did Plantation Houston East Bank Demerara go from cane estate to black gold field? **John Mair** explains

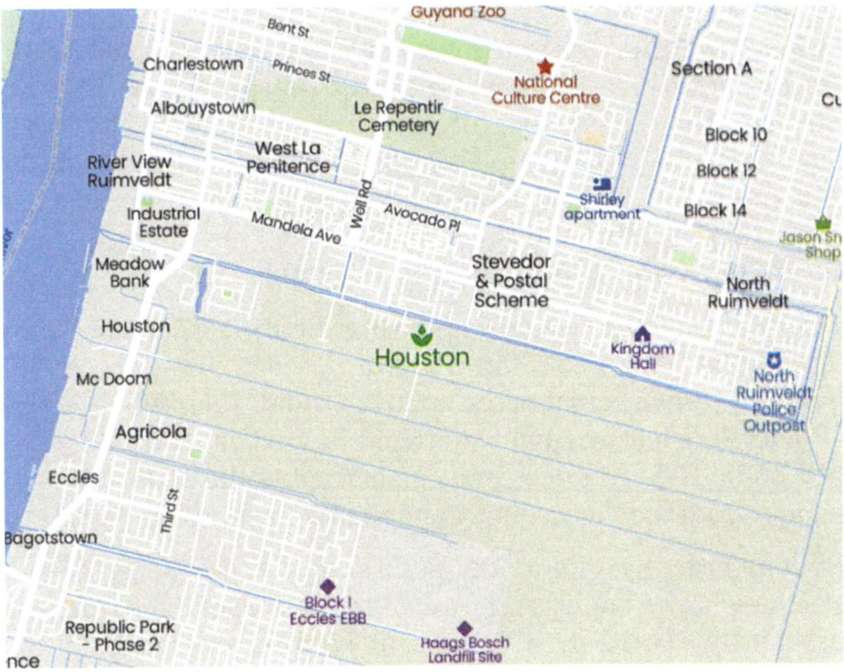

Source: Mapcarta

Plantation Houston. East Bank Demerara. It was a small family sugar estate of 1,600 acres in the Georgetown suburbs producing insufficient cane to keep their own factory grinding. Today the 500 acres of former cane field still left in the Vieira family are, almost literally, a gold field.

How did those fields become such a money tree?

Shore Base Central

Today, Houston in Guyana is the epicentre of the oil bonanza, replete with shore supply bases for the deep-sea offshore oil industry, still mainly ExxonMobil. It is just six miles from the mouth of the Demerara River, situated before the barrier of the Demerara Harbour Bridge which, when built in 1976, was deemed the world's longest floating bridge (LFSB). Local wags turned the initialism to the Linden Forbes Sampson Bridge in ironic tribute to the dictator LFS Burnham whose prize project it was.

In 2023, the entire river frontage in Houston is occupied by big world names like Schlumberger and the (Guyanese-fronted) Guyana Shore Base Inc (GSYBI). They supply the offshore industry with provisions, assembly, repairs, and much more, and receive, in return, from the floating production offshore ships, their detritus, mud, and garbage of all sorts to turn it into something more environmentally acceptable.

The Houston River frontage is at a premium. GSYBI alone claims to have invested US$150m there in the last five years. GSYBI paid US$18m for eight acres in 2019. Today, their whole site is 170 acres. Their original waterfront has expanded to 32 acres plus some 104 acres across the main road — the eastern side — bought from the Vieira family and their Houston sugar estate.

Schlumberger next door occupies a similar space. To get to that size they have bought land from others. Some of their land was previously owned by a prominent Indo-Guyanese family the Rahamans. That was a timber facility: Caribbean Timbers. Land was also bought from a local Indo hardware baron, Sataur Gafoor, who moved his wholesale premises lock stock and barrel down the road. Ironically, he bought that land from Houston estate to re-site it. A wharf owned by Eddy Vieira was sold to Totaltec a Guyanese/ American oil support company.

Houston Riverside is a modern version of Oil Monopoly.

It surely cannot be long before today's oil barons colonise the adjacent Demerara Sugar Terminal, the long-established export hub for the country's slow dying sugar industry.

The Vieira dynasty

How did the Vieiras come to be in this fortunate position? Family money, good husbandry, and happenstance. It was started by Manoel Senior who bought himself out of indentureship and set up a liquor business (in Guyanese parlance a rum shop) in Anna Caterina West Coast Demerara. It made money. Plenty. Enough to set up his family well.

Houston estate, the first to be owned in the 'colony' by a local Guyanese family, was bought in 1903 by Manoel Vieira Junior. He came from that old Portuguese/Guianese landed family.

After a spell in the liquor business, Manoel Junior went into the Guianese interior and prospected for diamonds with huge success.

Houston Plantation goes native

With the proceeds of that, Vieira bought Plantation Houston. His son Joseph Vieira, who was interested from an early age in agriculture, took over running the family estate in 1944 and, in time, he became one of the best and most profitable planters in 'BG'. His husbandry and profit-making skills were mellowed by Roman Catholic philanthropy learned from his Salesian education in the UK.

The family invested well and it bore results in the crops and more.

Joe Vieira was one of the great planters, full of ideas. But his estate's crops were not large enough to maintain its own grinding factory. That had to be closed in 1955. The sugar estate struggled on post-Independence through hostility from Presidents Burnham and Hoyte.

Raw materials become increasingly expensive as they were bought on the black market. Their sugar had to be sold on the white market. Houston still turned a profit on that. Joe's skills kept the sugar business going until it became firmly unprofitable and was abandoned in 2010, five years after his death. The next generation lost interest in sugar. The family had gone through some very hard times. Some of the land in Houston had to be sold off to pay off debts to Banks Breweries and some to Guysuco in Versailles (another Vieira plantation).

Away from core sugar, some of the Vieiras went into riverside businesses. A small shipyard was established in 1981 as well as an allied machinery supply business plus a fish processing business.

Up to 2010, the sugar estate had continued in its area limited way. Their fields were right up against sprawling Georgetown and boxed in by new EBD communities like Eccles and McDoom. Their fertile land was eyed up by many for decades.

The proceeds from the non-sugar enterprises were small fry compared with the riches when the oil boom came calling from 2017 onwards.

Oil Dorado comes to Houston

The Vieira family got into that phenomenon early with sales of land on the eastern side of the public road that crossed their estate.

Real estate came calling too. In 2019, Houston Estate sold 52 acres for housing to Redstart Investments, a half Guyanese company. Today, those former fields are luxury condos. The drainage canal, vital to cane cultivation, was filled in during the same year. Cane sugar cultivation was firmly no more at Plantation Houston after a century and more. Oil Dorado was to be the Vieira family future.

A traveller in time, even from the recent past, would not recognise Houston today. The change in the last decade is immense: huge warehouses, ritzy blocks of flats, either built or planned with expensive rents of US$3,000-5,000 per month. From the air you can just see the green remains of the sugar estate fields on the eastern side of the shore bases. A new highway just being built from urban Georgetown to suburban Diamond — with oil money — cuts through the remnants of the

Houston estate. That makes those 500 acres even more valuable.

But it has not been all plain sailing within the Vieira dynasty. Two cousins of the current family group, Houston residents Vanda and Danuta Radzik, took it upon themselves in 2022 to sue Schlumberger for storing radioactive material on their site, having, say the Radziks, railroaded through permission from the Environment Protection Agency without proper investigation. They won their case in the High Court in December 2022 and, for now, have put a stop to that. The EPA accepted the Court decision.

Houston East Bank Demerara is a metaphor for the metamorphosis of Guyana from a mono-crop sugar economy, in colonial and post-colonial times, to the oil bonanza of the last five years. The big old Portuguese and Indian families like the Vieiras, the Fernandes, the Gafoors, and The Muneshwers saw that future and bought into it. Lock, stock, and oil barrel.

What happens to the last 500 acres of those former sugar cane fields is a portent for Guyana's future. Sugar is dead, oil is alive. It is unlikely that the Vieira dynasty will lose out.

About the contributor

To declare interests, I am child of sugar. My father planted five miles down the East Bank Road from Houston on a British-owned estate in the 1950s. He managed Peter's Hall. I grew up there. I am also a long-standing personal friend of Anthony Vieira. He contributed to this piece.

Chapter Sixteen

Exxon's in the money. Honestly?

Not everyone in Guyana sings from the same hymn sheet. **GHK Lall** is what the Guyanese call a 'Come-backee' — a returnee from a life as a Wall Street banker to his native land and to the position of constant gadfly to ExxonMobil and the current government

America's oil power ExxonMobil has raked in the profits from its Guyana oil investment. Exxon's CEO, Darren Woods has himself spoken of how much the Guyana projects mean to his company, and the facts and visions are there to back him up: 'I mean if you look at this, it's really a story of success'. Liam Mallon, President of Exxon Upstream Company, describes developments in Guyana as 'absolutely unique', and unmatched in his 40 years with mega-projects globally. 'A story of success' and 'absolutely unique' emphasise the unprecedentedly rich and rewarding.

Exxon's partner in the Guyana venture, Hess Corporation, has reaped its share of rich returns from its participation in Offshore Oil Guyana, and the company's actions prove that it is riding high on the Guyana tide. The Chinese operate on a different wavelength, which means there is some haze and static in deciphering what it does with its take from Guyana's oil. Against the reports of glittering returns from Guyana's Stabroek Basin, the favourable analysts' commentaries, and the projections of venerable international agencies like the World Bank and the IMF, there are the Guyanese people languishing somewhere in the footnotes of the consortium's financial statements, as if they are secondary, almost an afterthought.

How much money?

In 2022 alone, the Stabroek Basin generated US$9.8bn in revenues, of which US$7.35bn first went to Exxon as partial recovery of its investment. Guyana's share out of that revenue generation was US$1.4bn, which means that Exxon's official share was equal to US$1.4bn less US$280m in royalties. What should be noted is that within the US$7.35bn deducted as return of capital invested, there would have been interest charges and deductions for decommissioning costs decades into the future.

Hundreds of millions of US dollars are being subtracted annually for clean-up expenses 20 years hence. In 2022, Asset Retirement Obligations (decommissioning) were listed at US$235m, an increase of 191 per cent. Those US$m will accumulate into US$bn when annualized. Exxon has the deducted aggregating millions under its control, which could be used to generate an income stream for the company. Even in escrow, it would be earning for ExxonMobil, and not Guyana. One thing is for sure, it is not sitting idle, for that is not the way of companies as sophisticated as Exxon.

How much invested?

Spotlighting interest charges to date, and considering only live oil production fields, Exxon has invested US$10bn at a minimum, and some of this is its own money, according to the company itself. Interest charges (part of the expenses claimed) could amount to close to US$1bn annually. Since Exxon was/is using its own money, then that is a hefty piece of its profit, but one about which the rate charged is unknown. When decommissioning costs are coupled with interest charges, these are significant (but unstated) additions to Exxon's profit pool from its Guyana oil operations.

Shell profits?

Importantly, in 2009 and 2011, Exxon released 25 per cent of the Stabroek Block to Shell plc, but those two likely rich financial events were off the books of both ExxonMobil and Shell, for they are nowhere to be seen. Half of the vast and potentially rich Stabroek Block was sublet to Shell plc, and there is neither revenue nor accounting entry noted in the company's records. In the normal course of events, those two farmouts should have resulted in revenue streams that are not insignificant, but

Exxon's accounting records are silent.

Holding in abeyance the possible deficits on Guyana's piece of those two actions, the two sales of material segments of the Stabroek Block had to have had a most positive impact on Exxon's overall profits from its oil operations and dealings in Guyana.

I take the position that the two transfer or special arrangements between Exxon and Shell could have been enough to offset completely Exxon's investments in the Stabroek Block at that time, and with possibly some gravy money ($USms) still left for the company to savour. Exxon is nothing if not a skilled dealer and among the toughest of bargainers to be found anywhere. Exxon is not in the philanthropy business; those sales-transfers-farmouts-subleases could not have been on the house. All things being equal, the two farmouts or carveouts of 25 per cent and 25 per cent of the Stabroek Block were sure to generate handsome up-front deposits from Shell to ExxonMobil for the privilege of working in a space as rich as Stabroek.

The point is that Exxon has made money at every twist and turn, and the company has spread the wealth among its own, through enrichment of its dividend, handsome executive suite compensation enhancement, and share buybacks. Additionally, the company has lifted itself out of an earlier slump in earnings, which has positioned it to venture into new projects, and Guyana's oil has been a consistent contributor of note. All told, Exxon seems to have done exceedingly well for itself, and this is probing beyond the company numbers, beyond the financial statements, and as evidenced in the pronouncements of its top executives from Darren Woods downwards.

Hess shouts

Whereas Exxon has maintained the public silhouette of corporate probity and executive subduedness, not so John Hess, CEO of Hess Corp, and a 30 per cent participant in the Exxon-led consortium. Hess Corp was in the doghouse of Wall Street analysts, but its returns from the investment in Guyana has prompted Mr Hess to get loquacious and generous. Like some slightly tipsy older uncle, CEO John Hess has been the epitome of what I term 'P-E-O', meaning, prattling extensively openly. The Hess chief cannot keep his mouth shut about how well his company has done in Guyana, how sweet the investment climate is, and how much the country means for the future of his company.

In 2022, powered by its handsome profits from Guyana's oil, Hess Corporation was able to reduce its debt by US$500m, buy back US$650m in shares, and increase its dividend by 50 per cent, which were all proudly announced by John Hess himself at a Barclays-sponsored energy gathering, saying, "More than 80 per cent of our 2023 budget is allocated to Guyana, which is positioned to be one of the highest-margin, lowest carbon intensity oil developments in the world, and to the Bakken."

In efforts to sell Hess Corporation to heavyweight investors, Mr Hess has been effusive and expansive in quarterly earnings calls before industry analysts, and at investor forums involving top Wall Street names, like JPMorgan Chase and others of that calibre. He sold out to Chevron in October 2023.

Chinese whispers

While Messrs Darren Woods and Alistair Routledge of ExxonGuyana have been circumspect about their Guyana oil motherlode, and John Hess has let the cat out of the bag, the third partner in the consortium, CNOOC, has comforted itself with refuge in silence. Little to nothing has been articulated publicly by CNOOC officials, but it can be safely concluded that its 25 per cent participation in the Stabroek Block has been a solid, if not spectacular, winner.

Guyana in the mix, but is Guyanese in a maze?

Amid the fanfare of fabulous GDP numbers for Guyana, and how richly the Exxon-led consortium is doing with its Guyana investment, there is the other side, the almost forgotten segment, of all the numbers and narratives. It has to do with what Guyana is getting for its massive oil and gas wealth. Amidst the combination of 2 per cent royalty and a 50-50 split in profits after 75 per cent of project costs are deducted up front from oil revenues, the Guyanese people, the owners of this wealth, are unhappy with where they are. The sentiment is that they should do better.

Citizens who object to this deal —made by the previous government — have been denounced and demonized, often criminalized by agents of the incumbent government for their pains, (as this writer can attest). The clamour from citizens, such as non-state analysts, independent commentators, and ordinary citizens, is for Exxon to do more for Guyana through a new contract that results from renegotiation of the 2016 document that is now generally reviled outside of official quarters.

2016 contract unfair to Guyana

Considering this, it is my position that Exxon stands to benefit hugely, if it were to be receptive to revisiting the 2016 Production Sharing Agreement (contract) and work out what is regarded as a straight deal, a clean deal. The present contract has too many money opportunities that are hidden, there are too many openings for Exxon to enhance its profits.

This is while Guyanese struggle with economic stresses, despite being labelled as the richest people per capita in the world. This is more than jarring to the hungry and empty-handed in Guyana, which is close to 50 per cent of the local population, according to the World Bank.

Is the current government in thrall to Exxon?

The current government of Guyana is said by some to be the handmaiden of the Exxon-spearheaded consortium, to the detriment of Guyanese interests. Examples of governmental acquiescence include the local Environment Protection Agency (EPA) reduced to a rubber stamp, new projects reviewed in extremely compressed times, and approved despite gaps in studies. Further still, Guyana currently has to depend on Exxon for reports on how much oil is produced daily, and how much gas is flared into the atmosphere.

Some Guyanese think that Exxon could do more for Guyana, without losing its earnings leadership in the non-governmental oil world, nor its path to more riches from the Stabroek Basin. It is better for Exxon to be seen as a partner and not as some old-line capitalist predator of the most despised sort: one that is out to gouge every penny for itself out of Guyana.

Sportswashing?

Exxon has satisfied itself with smoothing roiled local waters with sponsorship of things such as Caribbean Premier League cricket and sporadic community funding; and Hess has initiated a partnership with Mt Sinai Hospital in New York for advanced medical assistance for Guyanese. These are positives but they are not enough. Not when consideration is given to the reported profits of the company, and what also is reasonably believed to form part of undocumented and declared earnings from covert sources, such as expenses and sales/sublets of parts of the Stabroek Block to Shell. The fact that Exxon has clouded these arrangements and its expenses in secrecy does not make it look well in the eyes of Guyanese.

Pressure appears to be building on the Guyana Government, and its attacks on conscientiously objecting Guyanese only worsen the situation. Exxon is best advised to surrender some percentage points (royalties, taxes, interest rate, and conditions). It would go a long way, and make Guyanese think and feel that in Exxon they have a fair and trusted partner.

About the contributor

GHK Lall was born in Guyana and is a columnist in the *Kaieteur News* and other Guyanese publications. He emigrated to the USA and is a former Wall Street banker who came back to Guyana to head the Guyana Gold Board under President David Grainger. He lost that job when Grainger lost the 2020 election.

Chapter Seventeen

The Anti-Oil Lobby (AOL)

Freddie Kissoon is one of the more trenchant newspaper columnists in Guyana. For over three decades he has trod the boards of the daily press. In the recent past he has written in the pro-government *Guyana Chronicle*. Kissoon has been coruscating is his view of the AOL - especially those living abroad. This is an edited selection by **John Mair** from Kissoon's thousands of words

'What we have in Guyana is the opposite of common sense. The newspapers' letter sections and social media commentaries are filled with foreign-based Guyanese who write on Guyana informing Guyanese who live here about things that happen here when they don't live here.

'There are anti-government critics living in and out of this country that are relentless in their condemnations of the policies and actions of the Guyana Government. It would be extremely unwise for one to even suggest that such people should be stopped. Free speech and other important values simply evaporate when society does not allow people to voice their dissension and disagreements over the use of power.

'Dr. Alissa Trotz has edited a column in *Stabroek News* titled 'In The Diaspora' (ITD) for over 10 years now. Not one, I repeat, no one contributor to ITD has been an independent political analyst or someone who sees the government with sympathetic eyes. All of the contributors of ITD have been people who view the Guyana Government in an unfavourable light.

'ITD columnist, Dr Percy Hitnzen laments our reliance on fossil fuel industry. He has been living in California for the past 40 years. A German Guyanese, Dr Andre Brandli gave us an account of the 2020 (attempted rigged) general election here and he wasn't a day in Guyana from March 2 to August 2 when the process concluded.'

Melinda Janki: campaigning lawyer?

Kissoon's ire is concentrated on a couple of major targets, one of whom, 'comebackee' lawyer Melinda Janki, is firmly anti-oil in Guyana:

'One of the persons against the continuation of the fossil fuel industry in Guyana is a woman named Melinda Janki. She has been given space by the two anti-government newspapers to make two points. One is that the contract between Exxon and the Guyana government can be renegotiated. Let's quote her, "Any law student knows the parties to a contract can always agree to change it."

'The other point is that she argues that the Guyanese people do not trust the government to be firm with Exxon.

'If Guyanese who want to see Guyana have a great economy do not reply to these untenable, misleading narratives of Janki and the usual suspects, then propaganda becomes effective. It is for this reason patriotic Guyanese must confront the dangerous thoughts of the anti-oil lobby. This column is a small contribution to that endeavour.

'There is no need to dwell on the flawed analogy between a normal contract and the agreement between Exxon and Guyana, so let's move to Janki's second point about the Guyanese people not putting any trust in the government in its relation with Exxon. Did Janki and the usual suspects do a poll to determine how the Guyanese people view the oil industry and if the Guyanese nation wants the country to stop oil production because of climate change?

'The Guyanese people know that the world needs oil and the world will buy Guyanese oil so Guyana can have income that can be used to dilute poverty and make Guyana a better place to live in. The other reason is that the Guyanese people do not trust personalities like Janki and the other anti-oil lobbyists because they feel that the anti-oil arguments is a political ploy to get at the government.

'In May 2018 Ms Janki in a deep British accent (Ms Janki lived a long time and still does in the UK). She asked the following question, and I am quoting her exact words "What will oil do for Guyana? The answer is oil will make Guyana poorer not richer."

'In her view, Guyana should not engage in oil production because the disaster accruing from an exploded well or oil spill will wipe out any gains and will make Guyana a crippled economy (my words) because recovery from such a disaster will not be an easy one Ms. Janki said this explains why we will not be richer but poorer.

'Civilisation has never paid any attention to such gloom and doom in looking at life for the reverse reason. If you cannot predict what life will bring then how can you abstain from building and inventing and acting? Crazy drivers kill people on the roads, then why travel in a car. Trains derail and people die, then why travel in a train. Untold numbers have died in plane crashes, why countries continue to manufacture planes.ms over the past hundreds years have been robbed while shopping, why go out and shop then?

'I advise you to listen to Ms Janki if you want to see with graphic potency what society in Guyana has to contend with today'.

The OGGN (Oil and Gas Governance Network)

Another regular target of Kissoon's ire in print is the OGGN based in the large Guyanese diaspora in the USA. First, the OGGN's self-declared genesis:

'In the summer of 2017, OGGN was created as a legitimate non-profit organization located in Hollis, New York, United States OGGN's mission is to advocate for the rule of law, transparency, good governance, and accountability with respect to oil exploration and production in Guyana.'

Kissoon on the OGGN: 'Let's examine the politics of OGGN more closely. Two statements force one to conclude that OGGN is either a hypocritical body or a comical outfit. The first statement is taken from the July 29, 2023 post on its website, it goes like this: "OGGN has no political association." For an organization that has no political association, it is always on the same wavelength with people who hate the government.

'Let's have more quotes from the July 29, 2023 publication; "Collectively, they have years of experience in business, industry, research, and/or academia. All of OGGN's directors work on a pro bono basis for the benefit of all Guyanese." Five questions arise here:

1. These people with their years of experience have given their skills to which countries and Guyana is included?
2. How long these experienced people lived in other foreign lands?
3. If they do not work on a pro- bono basis, then who in Guyana or elsewhere they expect to pay them for writing about Guyana's oil industry while living in someplace named Hollis in the United States?
4. Where are the benefits OGGN bring to Guyana? Who in Guyana knows OGGN? '

'I find it inscrutable that a group of Guyanese who all may be citizens of foreign countries and do not contribute to the contents of Guyana in anyway, has organized themselves to speak on behalf of the population here. Well, that may not be a caricature in itself but it becomes a caricature when that body never consulted Guyanese who live here about if we want them to represent us'.

Kissoon is never one to mince his words.

Professor Clive Thomas agrees with Kissoon about the AOL

Kissoon is an iconoclast. Never afraid to be in a minority of one. On the folly of the AOL, he has recently found a powerful ally. Professor Clive Thomas is a Guyanese economist of some standing and an office-holder in the previous regime. Thomas is not a supporter of the current government. Kissoon on Thomas:

'Thank you Clive Thomas, for now joining me! To date, only five persons (outside of governmental circles) have publicly condemned the advocacy of some politically-driven, unpatriotic minds that want Guyana to reject oil production because they say fossil fuel industry is not climate-friendly.

'In the November 13, 2022 issue of the *Stabroek News*, a letter appeared demanding that the government discontinue oil production. The signatures used the word, "immediate."

'Here are two words Thomas used to describe the attitude of people who want Guyana to stop oil production – "crass inhumanity." He based his contempt of these people and the class they belong on three points.

1. The income from the oil industry is crucial for the elimination of poverty and the eradication of poverty should be uppermost in the mind of all Guyanese.
2. The middle class cannot call for the removal of the oil industry when the lives of the middle class are replete with resources that come from the oil industry.
3. You cannot ask Guyana alone to save the environment.'

Oil leads to strange bedfellows all over the world especially in Guyana.

Why the AOL is wrong

Kissoon's positions on what he calls 'the usual suspects' and their effect:

'If the AOL wins these frivolous court cases (against Big Oil) then four things happen and the entire nation of Guyana must understand this.

'1) the country loses a form of income never before seen in the entire history of Guyana stretching back to early colonial times and this will have unimaginable consequences for poverty reduction and developmental planning.

'2) no foreign company will see Guyana as a reliable place to pursue investments. The judge's words hint at that when she spoke of the consequences to Guyana was she to accept the AOL's arguments. All judges, in all three tiers of Guyana's legal jurisdiction (High Court, Court of Appeal and CCJ) in future

AOL's writs will consider the impact of the entirety of Guyana existence before they stop oil investments in Guyana.

'3) powerful foreign governments that have been Guyana's closest allies since Independence will subtly move away from its traditional friendship with this country.

'4) the closing down of the oil industry will create political and economic conditions that will allow for instability thereby opening up possibilities for AOL and their mulatto/Creole class to attempt to possess political power.'

In the end ... Freddie Kissoon

'In conclusion, I am arguing that the anti-oil lobby is essentially a class elitist outfit that has atavistically reverted to its pristine self in the 1940 where it saw the Indian politically challenge to be extirpated with urgency. The anti-oil lobby is essentially a continuation of the League of Coloured People and its party, the National Democratic Party. I refer to this stratum in my ongoing daily column as the mulatto/Creole class (MCC).

'With the defeat of the PPP government in 2015, them MCC had finally achieved power having a slight taste of it under the United Force in 1964-1968. Them MCC embraced the 2015 APNU+AFC regime because that government came from the womb of them MCC with people like David Granger, his ministers Rupert Roopnarine, Raphael Trotman and Cathy Hughes.

'The APNU+AFC's election defeat in 2020 has left them MCC is a horrible psychological state. This explains why all the members of the anti-oil lobby did not condemn the five months of election rigging between March and July in 2020. The anti-oil lobby, I need to stress is not anti-oil at all. If Granger had returned to power, there would have been no anti-oil lobby. What them MCC is doing is using the Exxon contract as their platform to weaken the PPP government because it is their only game in town. With the increasing popularity of President Ali and a national budget that allows for the attenuation of poverty, there is no other platform that them MCC could find to appeal to the Guyanese people.

'This appeal has floundered because the Guyanese people know that income from oil has guaranteed a national income that has long eluded Guyana. It is put best by Professor Clive Thomas who described the anti-oil lobby as engaging in "crass inhumanity." Thomas argues that at last Guyana has the resources to make huge dents into Guyana's perennial poverty. He is right.

About the contributor

Frederick 'Freddie' Kissoon was educated at the University of Guyana, MacMaster University, and the University of Toronto. He taught for 26 years at the University of Guyana and has been a featured columnist with all the major newspapers in Guyana. He currently writes a daily column in the *Guyana Chronicle* and hosts the popular social media interview programme – the *Freddie Kissoon-Gildarie Show*.

Chapter Eighteen

All that glisters is not gold: The CGX story

John Mair tells the sad tale of a first mover that may become a first outer

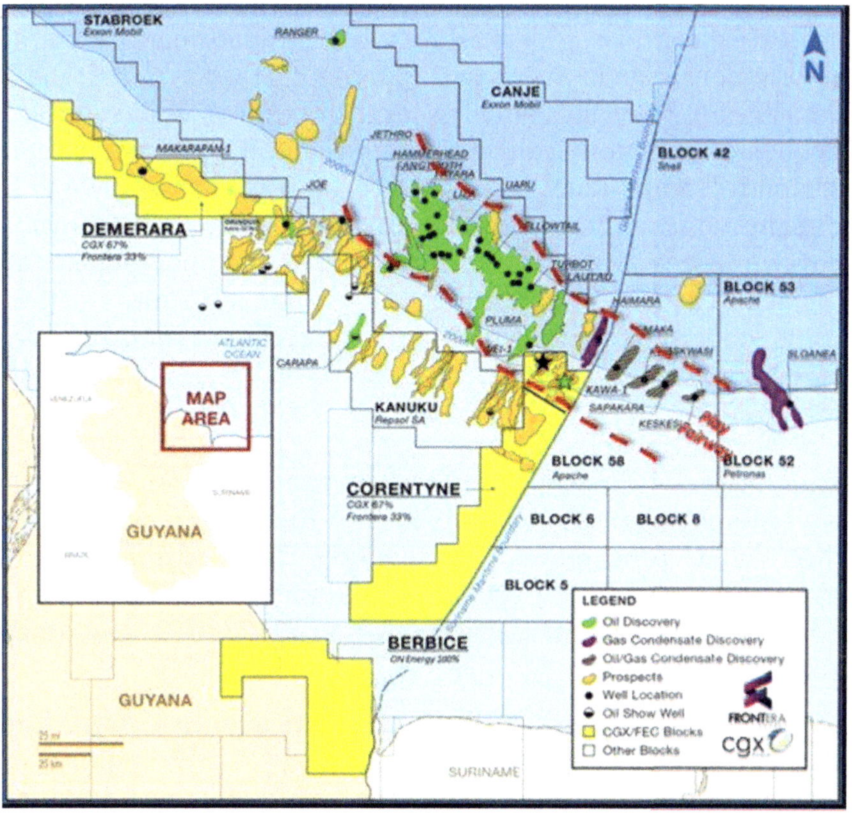

Source: CGX

CGX should be one of the major success stories of the Guyana oil boom. They are not, and like the Black Knight in *Monty Python and the Holy Grail* who has every limb hacked off bit by bit, they are having to sell off limb after limb to others to stay in the oil exploration business. It seems a sad story. How did they get there

Let's go back to Guyana oil pre-history. 1998. The company was formed in Canada by John Cullen and Guyanese émigré Idres K Dookie. CGX were the first movers in Guyana oil. In June 2000 they set up an exploratory rig in the disputed area between Guyana and Suriname. They were chased off by the Surinamese navy. That caused great regional tension. I was working for then President Jagdeo at the time and experienced it first-hand. The chickens were losing their heads. Guyana had (and still has) no navy to speak of so, instead, they took the Surinam Bouterse government to an international court, citing the Laws of the Seas Convention. They engaged high-level and expensive lawyers, led by former Commonwealth Secretary General and Guyanese Sir Shridath 'Sonny' Ramphal. That litigation is said to have cost US$5m, with finance allegedly provided by CGX. The Guyana government won the case in 2007. Under the final judgement, Guyana was given 93 per cent of the area under dispute and they could start thinking of exploiting that section of their offshore oil resources.

Jagdeo grateful?

Then President Jagdeo, today the Guyana oil supremo, and his government were deeply indebted to them. They were given three areas to explore with the New Demerara Petroleum Agreement, the New Berbice Petroleum Agreement and the Corentyne Petroleum Agreement in 2012/2013 (see map above).

CGX continued to try to find commercial oil offshore and onshore, but they were still late to the party and oil-finding is an expensive business. Two wells were drilled on their Corentyne block licence Another well, Jaguar-1, was drilled in February 2012 on the Georgetown block but was subsequently abandoned due to safety concerns. Eagle-1 was drilled months later, but the results there too were disappointing.

All costs and no revenue so far for CGX.

What CGX had:

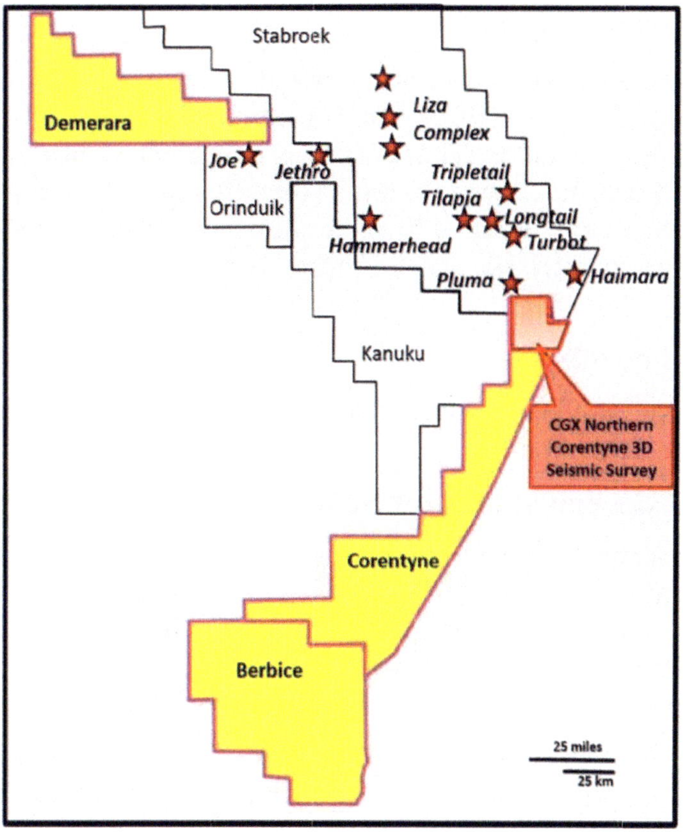

Source: CGX

Turbulence above the surface

CGX itself meanwhile was going through ructions. Founder Idris K Dookie, by now an almost permanent feature at Pegasus Hotel poolside in Georgetown entertaining clients (this author noted he had two mobile phones which he certainly regarded as 'interesting'. Today he can be found next door in the classier Marriott), was deposed in a palace coup in March 2013. In 2022, he is still bitter at what he told me were 'the traitors'.

CGX itself soldiered on whilst admitting they were in dire financial straits. One company, Pacific Rubales Energy, was being offered 70 per cent of CGX in return for a capital infusion of $15m. That deal did not materialise.

Boom but bust for CGX

The Guyana oil boom proper did not start until May 2015 when ExxonMobil struck oil big in the Stabroek field. CGX had licences in the adjacent fields. Those were proving fallow but, despite that, CGX continued exploring and spending money in pursuit of the oil Holy Grail. By now the company had a new chair/CEO in Professor Suresh Narine, a young tyro Canadian/Guyanese academic.

But still no oil

Turbulence and new brooms in the boardroom did not bring any better results offshore.

Light at the end of the tunnel: Jagdeo still grateful?

In February 2022, just in time for the biggest oil/gas conference ever held in Guyana, CGX finally struck oil at the Kawi well in their Corentyne block. It came with a cost. To fund the further exploration of the Wei-1 well and Kawi wells they had to relinquish shares in the company to Frontera Energy.

In return for $160m of injected capital CGX gave up two-thirds of the company. Some of that amount was repayment for monies borrowed on convertible loans from Frontera in 2021 and 2022. The deal meant that Frontera became the operator of the Corentyne licence with a 68 per cent stake, while CGX retained the remaining 32 per cent working interest.

More limbs sacrificed

It was said that Bharrat Jagdeo, now the oil supremo, was losing patience with his erstwhile friends. In June 2022 he announced that, given their inability to honour their work obligations, Frontera Energy Corporation and CGX Energy Inc. had reached an agreement with the Guyana government to relinquish the Demerara and Berbice Blocks, amounting to a combined 1.1m acres. Two-thirds gone.

More limbs amputated. But oil was on its way. Was it?

Drilling of Wei-1 exploration well was set to take place in October 2022. That deadline kept slipping towards the middle of 2023.

Twenty-two years on: Diversification?

CGX today is operator of just the Corentyne block. Partners Frontera Energy Corporation hold a two-thirds interest while CGX hold just a third interest. It was still not all plain sailing to profit from oil though. CGX announced that the opening-up of the Wei-1 well had shifted from quarter three to quarter four in 2022 to later. It is thought for financial/cost flow reasons.

Twenty years and no commercial oil to date. Losses were mounting. CGX Energy Inc announced on 10 August that for the first half of the year 2022 it has recorded almost US$7m in losses. compared with a net loss of US $3.4m for the same period in 2021. CGX were quite simply running out of limbs to sacrifice.

One last delay?

Suresh Narine had also proudly announced at that February 2022 conference the building by CGX of a deepwater port in Berbice (BDWP). He showed the audience detailed plans for it. The deepwater port facility is intended to serve as an offshore supply base for the oil and gas industry and as a multi-purpose terminal cargo handling base to service agricultural import/export, containerised, and specialized cargo. The BDWP aims to enable provisioning of operators and vendors in territorial waters of both Guyana and Suriname.

But today even that sideshow looks like going sour as Guyana President Ali told the company in August 2022 to get a move on with that project or lose it. He had other investors waiting on the sidelines ready and willing to build the facility and to profit from it. CGX announced in the same month that the building of that deepwater port was behind schedule. To date, they have spent US$22m on the BDWP. It has yet to open. See below.

Not quite the end

On 1 December 2022, in another new announcement CGX said it was postponing drilling of the Wei-1 well in offshore Guyana, citing contractor obligations elsewhere. They said they had agreed with the Guyanese government to start drilling no later than 31 January 2023 to allow contractor Noble Corp Plc to complete their current obligations in Trinidad.

They did explore in early 2023 and they did find oil in Wei which they announced with much fanfare in June 2023. But, and it is always a but with CGX/Frontera, they announced in August 2023 that they needed two to three months of analysis to decide whether the find was significant and commercial. Results are still awaited in October 2023.

The Berbice deepwater port is equally mired in mystery. Construction has begun but Vice President Bharat Jagdeo said in August 2023 that while the port being built in Berbice by oil and gas company CGX Energy Inc was being dubbed a deepwater port, it was not. He explained that the port the company was building was a regular port and will support oil and gas activities. Two weeks later, President Ali announced that the Government of Guyana was conducting a feasibility study for a real deepwater port. Privately financed, not by CGX, and not in Berbice!

In the game of chess that is Guyana's oil politics, CGX/Frontera seem to be getting close to checkmate.

The future onshore is therefore not bright. Offshore there is a little more hope. From oil heroes to oil near zeroes in two decades. Few limbs are left to amputate. The body now belongs to others. It may be just a corpse. That sadly, is the CGX story.

SECTION TWO : LESSONS FROM NEAR AND AFAR

Introduction

John Mair

My own long-term interest in Guyana – I was born there – and oil was the spur for this book's five previous editions. In this sixth edition of the book, I and others explore some more lessons for the new petro-state. The learnings for Guyana are as much geopolitical as economic.

As Guyana goes from nothing to world oil power in a decade, what can the country learn from others with oil riches? In this section, we look at the experiences in six other oil kingdoms: two near neighbours, Trinidad and Tobago, and Venezuela, and Scotland, Ghana, Texas USA, and Kazakhstan.

'Dax' Driver, from the Trinidad and Tobago Energy Chamber, gives an up-to-date picture of what Guyana can learn from his country in a piece specially written for this book. The Trinis, whose oil and gas is running out and who have closed their refinery, look enviously to Guyana for their future Trinidad oil experts, and businesses are already starting to colonise the Guyana oil scene – not without demur. Driver offers five lessons from Trinidad and Tobago's century of oil. In his words, 'Trinidad and Tobago have many lessons it can offer to Guyana, the world's most exciting new hydrocarbon province. This includes both things to emulate and things to avoid'.

Venezuela has gone from petro-state to pariah state. I look at how Geoffrey Da Silva was Guyana Ambassador to Venezuela from 2011 to 2015. He offers his perspective on the troublesome neighbour.

Greg Quinn has served a senior British diplomat in both Guyana and Kazakhstan. Both are new oil territories. He gives his unique perspective on the comparatives. Nick Vacarro in the USA examines the infrastructural and allied problems brought by an oil boom. Former Lord Provost Barney Crockett reports from the UK's own Oil Dorado - Aberdeen - on lessons learned there for Guyana.

Finally, a pair of perspectives from Africa, Ghana in particular. Stanley Amerteifio, who heads the trade body for Ghanaians in Guyana, puts a positive spin on their oil experience. In my chapter, I try to sprinkle a touch of realism on the Ghana oil journey.

There are plenty of templates - positive and negative - from around the world for Oil Dorado to follow or to avoid.

They decide.

Chapter Nineteen

Lessons for Guyana from Trinidad and Tobago (2022)

Thackwray (Dax) Driver, President and CEO of the Energy Chamber of Trinidad and Tobago, offers five lessons of his country's hundred years of experience in oil and gas to its neighbour, the world's most exciting new hydrocarbon province

Trinidad and Tobago is one of the world's oldest hydrocarbon producers, with commercial oil production starting in 1908 and commercial gas production starting in 1953. With over a century of experience, Trinidad and Tobago has many lessons it can offer to Guyana, the world's most exciting new hydrocarbon province. This includes both things to emulate and things to avoid.

1. Remain open to international investors

Trinidad and Tobago has always been open to direct foreign investment in its hydrocarbon industry. While state-owned companies play an important role, Trinidad and Tobago has avoided the temptation to expropriate foreign-owned assets and has carefully guarded its reputation for respecting the sanctity of contracts and adhering to investment agreements. This has been a major strength for the country and has meant that investors have remained confident in investing in the country, even though our resource base has not been as impressive as some others.

There have been times when the agreements signed with foreign investors did not, with hindsight, turn out to give the best possible value to Trinidad and Tobago. In those cases, the government has sometimes sought to renegotiate but this must always be done by mutual consent and not unilaterally imposed. Contracts have an end-date and governments have an opportunity to renegotiate at the end of contract periods. Once investors lose trust in a jurisdiction it is very difficult to win it back. Expropriation of assets and unilateral imposition of new contracts may be politically popular in the short term, but it inevitably ends in disaster.

2. Make decisions quickly when things change

The international energy industry is always in a state of flux. Technology and markets always change and can change quickly. Trinidad and Tobago's liquefied natural gas (LNG) industry was built in the 1990s and 2000s on the demand for imported gas in the United States. The 'shale gas revolution', based on the application of fracking technology, totally changed the shape of the gas industry and the US is now the world's leading LNG exporter. As the global industry changes, countries must shift their strategy and change their policies and regulations.

While we have generally been able to change our approach as the global industry has changed, we have sometimes been slow to take decisions. For example, Trinidad and Tobago has been slow to make changes to the windfall taxation system for crude oil production put in place in 1981 during the first oil boom. This windfall tax was designed to kick in when oil prices averaged above US$50 per barrel as a way of ensuring a fair share of revenue for the government. Unfortunately, the threshold price was not inflation-linked and the windfall tax still kicks in at $50, which is certainly not considered high today. This has acted as a disincentive to investment in crude oil production and has significantly contributed to the decline in activity and oil production over the past two decades (the tax is not levied against natural gas). While the issue associated with this tax has been identified repeatedly, it has been difficult to amend a system which delivers short-term revenue to the government, even though it dampens long-term investment.

While the industry in Guyana has a very rosy future at present, the government should always be ready to quickly make decisions if circumstances change. Being able to respond quickly to changing circumstances is important to long-term success. This means having nimble and responsive policy-making systems within the government.

3. Invest in training and skills development

Trinidad and Tobago has invested heavily in education, training, and skills development. This has created a cadre of skilled leaders, professionals, technicians, and skilled workers. While the energy sector has always been open to international investors and international service companies and contractors, most workers in the industry are nationals or permanent residents. The Energy Chamber tracks the nationality of all workers in the petrochemical, LNG, and heavy industrial sector (through our administration of the basic safety assessments for all workers). In 2021, 99 per cent of the workers in this sub-sector were Trinidad and Tobago nationals or permanent residents. This has been consistent since we started tracking the nationality of workers a decade ago, with around 16,000 individuals per annum undergoing the assessment.

The University of the West Indies has produced a lot of the leaders in the energy industry, including many petroleum engineers and geologists, but also lawyers, accountants, and other professionals. Many other leaders went to international universities on government scholarships before returning to Trinidad. More recently, the University of Trinidad and Tobago has produced many graduates with strong practical experience and skills, filling important managerial and technical roles.

Historically, many skilled labourers came out of company apprentice systems and the skilled technicians and craft workers produced through these programmes formed the backbone of the industry during the 1970s, 1980s, and 1990s. With the shift to more services being contracted out to service companies, more of the skilled labour force has come through institutions such as the NESC Technical Institute and the Kenson School of Production Technology. Service companies and contractors have also often developed robust in-house training programmes.

One area in which we could have done more in training and development is in the adoption of competency-based assessments that provide certification for skilled workers who have learned on the job. There are many skilled workers who do not possess the certificates to show that they are competent, and this hampers their ability to move up in organisations or to work internationally. This is an area in which Guyana and Trinidad and Tobago could cooperate for mutual benefit and ensure that as workers gain practical skills, they also get competency-based certification against the Caribbean Vocational Qualification (CVQ) system.

Nevertheless, the investments that Trinidad and Tobago has made in education and skills development means that we do have many nationals working in the oil and gas industry outside of the country. You would be hard-pressed to find an oilfield or an LNG facility anywhere in the world without a Trinidadian working there. Of course, there are many skilled and experienced Trinidadians now working in Guyana.

4. Invest in creating a safety culture

Trinidad and Tobago's energy sector has developed a robust safety culture and the safety record in the industry has generally been good, though this cannot ever lead to complacency. The safety performance of many of the offshore operators and downstream process facilities has compared well in international benchmarking exercises.

The safety culture within the energy sector has developed in a context of generally weak national safety regulatory enforcement and industry leaders have had to work hard to keep a strong focus on safety in this environment. Through the Safe to Work programme (STOW), the Energy Chamber has played a role in developing the industry safety culture with a particular focus on contractor safety management. This award-winning scheme has created an industrywide uniform HSE pre-qualification programme with over 2,200 audits having been conducted and 750 companies having been certified against the STOW requirements.

STOW has shown how industry standards can help build a strong safety culture through industry self-regulation, rather than having to rely on regulation from the state. These experiences can be easily transferred to Guyana.

5. Be very careful with subsidies

Like many other hydrocarbon-producing economies, Trinidad and Tobago has shielded citizens from international fuel and electricity prices through subsidies. This means that citizens have enjoyed some of the world's cheapest electricity rates with gasoline and diesel prices typically at much lower rates than in other Caribbean countries. LPG or cooking gas has also been heavily subsidised and is very cheap compared with most countries.

While citizens obviously benefit from these subsidised prices (though surprisingly still often complain) the subsidy system has led to some serious distortions and poor social, economic, and environmental outcomes. When the transport fuel subsidy was originally set up it was to be paid for through a levy on oil companies, but as car ownership and hence fuel use increased and then, as oil production decreased, the government had to step in to pay for the subsidy directly from central government funds. Over the decades, billions of dollars of government funds have gone into keeping fuel prices low. This is effectively a transfer of funds to better-off households, who typically own more than one private motor vehicle and who use most fuel.

The subsidy has also led to high levels of car ownership and debilitating traffic jams that seriously affect people's mental and physical health and national productivity. With the benefit of hindsight, if the billions of dollars of funding for gasoline and diesel had instead been funnelled into investments in public transport, Trinidad and Tobago would have had a world-class public transport system and a healthier and happier population. Having created the current system, however, it is very difficult and politically unpopular to implement a new model for mobility. Guyana would do well to avoid this problem in the first place by not subsidising transport fuels and investing heavily in public transport.

Trinidad and Tobago's electricity is almost 100 per cent produced by natural gas power generation. The electricity subsidy is effectively provided by the gas industry, who are contractually obligated to provide a tranche of gas at prices well below market rates to that sector. This gas for electricity accounts for about 10 per cent of current total gas production. With very low electricity prices, the population is typically not very conscious of wasting electricity and a lot of energy is wasted. Trinidad and Tobago is very energy-inefficient. This means that gas that could be channelled to export-earning sectors like LNG, methanol, or ammonia is instead simply wasted.

There are excellent social and economic reasons for ensuring that every single household can access electricity as well as a good argument for making this available at a subsidised rate. It makes sense to subsidise the small amount of electricity needed for lights, a fridge, and a fan or two. It does not make sense to subsidise flat-screen TVs, central air conditioning, and pool pumps for the richest households. It is the richest households who use most of the electricity and it is these households who should be incentivised to be more energy-efficient, by making sure that they pay market prices for their electricity.

Smart meters mean that it is easy to put in a place a rate system along these lines and Guyana should be investing heavily in its grid and metering system, at the same time as it is embarking on its gas-to-electricity project. Once subsidies are implemented across the board, they are politically very difficult to remove, and Guyana would do well to avoid this problem in the first place.

There are, of course, many other lessons that Guyana could learn from Trinidad and Tobago and the Energy Chamber is always open to sharing our knowledge and understanding. Our countries and energy industries are closely intertwined, and I am sure that we will also have a lot to learn from Guyana, as the Guyanese oil industry continues its unprecedented rise.

About the contributor

Dr Thackwray Driver, better known as Dax, has been the President and CEO of the Energy Chamber of Trinidad and Tobago for the past twenty years. He oversaw the transformation of the organisation from a regional chamber in South Trinidad to a national trade association representing companies from across the energy value chain, from small family-owned contractors through to major multi-nationals and state-owned oil and gas companies. He has a PhD in environmental history from the University of London.

Chapter Twenty

Lessons from Venezuela 1: Pariah

Venezuela has the biggest oil reserves in the world but the lessons of the last two decades have not all been good ones. **John Mair** argues that Venezuela has gone from petro-power state to poor pariah state

Guyana shares a disputed border with the Bolivarian Republic of Venezuela. It is a fractious relationship. Put simply, Venezuela has laid claim to a third of Guyana for the last century and more. That case is currently before the International Court of Justice in the Hague.

Before 2015, Guyana was also the poor oil neighbour of the Bolivarian republic.

Venezuela in South America is at the mercy of faraway geopolitics. Made by the USA, then unmade by them, then 'saved' by Russia, and now in the process of being 'saved' anew by Uncle Sam, all thanks to Russia's 2022 invasion of Ukraine, and the West being desperate for new energy sources.

In the beginning, Venezuela was fully qualified to become a titan of the global oil industry. One of the founding members of the Organization of the Petroleum Exporting Countries (OPEC), the South American nation holds the largest crude oil reserves in the world, amounting to more than 300bn barrels.

With an annual crude oil production of more than three million barrels per day, Venezuela was once, along with Mexico, one of the two largest oil-producing countries in Latin America. Eight per cent of their exports were oil, and that figure rose to a whopping 96 per cent in 2013.

It was a country based on oil: huge amounts, mainly exported to the USA. Surely nothing could go wrong, could it?

The socialist revolution

They called it the Bolivarian Revolution in honour of the 19th century national hero Simón Bolivar. Hugo Chavez seized power in the 1999 army coup and, on his death in 2013, his successor Nicholas Maduro imposed a brand of harsh socialism on the country. The oil industry was nationalised and much more too. The rich fled, mainly to the USA. Florida is Caracas in exile. Venezuela went from hero to zero in the eyes of the USA,

Chavez's version of socialism may have been popular with the struggling masses in what had been a very unequal society, but it became a rogue state to the USA, especially to the very right-wing Trump regime from 2016. They accused the Maduro regime of fiddling elections and even went as far as to recognise the Opposition leader Juan Gaudio as the 'real' President in 2019.

Nevertheless, gradually increasing economic sanctions imposed by the US government since 2017 put further strains on Venezuela's oil sector. Where the US had previously been the leading destination for Venezuelan oil exports, by mid-2019 trade with the US came to a complete halt. The sanctions were eased in 2023.

The sector was kept going as a long-distance satellite of Putin's Russia and various contra deals in the Caribbean as part of the Petro Caribe strategy. Guyana, for example, traded rice for oil.

How far did they fall?

Nowadays, however, after nearly two decades of persistent decline in output, the country has dropped to fourth-biggest producer in the region, overtaken by Brazil and Colombia. In early 2022, Venezuela's monthly crude output reached an average of 700 thousand barrels of oil per day. While this represented a year-on-year growth, production had declined by more than 70 per cent in comparison with output a decade earlier.

Venezuelan refinery production has dipped below 200,000 barrels per day in the past three years, roughly 15 per cent of its refining capacity. As a result, shortages of fuels such as gasoline (for years heavily subsidised by the government and considered by its citizens a birthright) have become a constant struggle. Petroleum is such an important lifeline for the nation that, even with the continual drop in production, Venezuela still managed to maintain an average of 1.7 million daily barrels of crude oil exports for most of the decade.

In addition to allegations of rigging the 2020 election, Maduro's government has been accused of crimes against humanity, including the authorising of gruesome torture and extrajudicial killings, according to a 2020 report from the United Nations human rights body. Previous rounds of negotiations between Maduro and his opposition had fallen through, including attempts in October 2021.

Venezuela was seemingly on its uppers. There were food queues but Maduro was still firmly in power.

Then came the invasion of Ukraine

As the result of economic sanctions aimed at forcing Maduro out of power, US companies were prohibited from conducting business with Venezuela's state-owned oil company since 2019 but Maduro remains President.

Talks between the US and Venezuela governments began in March 2022. This was one month after Russia's invasion of Ukraine as US President Joe Biden began searching for alternatives to Russian oil and the US looked to weaken Russia's economy as the war dragged on.

The Biden administration granted a licence in November 2022 to Chevron to resume oil production in Venezuela, easing sanctions imposed on the country in 2019 over corruption and human rights concerns. This licence comes with several limitations, however, including a provision prohibiting Chevron from conducting any transactions with Iran or Russian-owned entities in Venezuela. It also prohibits the country's nationalised oil company, Petroleos de Venezuela, SA, which the US sanctioned in 2019, from receiving profits from Chevron's oil sales, which are intended to go instead to repaying debts owed to Chevron.

The lessons for Guyana

So, from petro power state to poor pariah state and now in by the back door, the lesson for Guyana from Venezuela is always keep on the right side of the big Eagle to the north. The Bear is not a substitute any more. This is the new Monroe Doctrine. Guyana seems to have learned that lesson and is hugger-mugger with the USA and ExxonMobil. The USA resolved the 2020 election 'fiddling' crisis in favour of the current government.

Chapter Twenty-One

Lessons from Venezuela 2: Politics

Guyana's 'noisy neighbour', the Bolivarian Republic of Venezuela, is 100 years ahead of it in the oil journey. It prospered, then it failed. Badly. Today it is a pariah state in much poverty. **Geoffrey Da Silva** was Guyana's Ambassador there from 2011 to 2015

How did Venezuela become infected with the oil 'Dutch Disease'? Today, after 95 years of oil production, and with presently the largest reserves of oil in the world at 300bn barrels, the Bolivarian Republic has failed to overcome several key challenges:

1. A very heavy dependence on oil exports for state revenues - about 90 per cent of all revenues are from oil exports.
2. A society very polarised along race and class lines - with a mainly White middle class and a small labour aristocracy who enjoy North American living standards and services (accommodation, restaurants, hotels) but where the majority of the population, who are Brown, Black, and Indigenous workers, farmers, the unemployed, and poor marginalised communities, have not experienced any sustainable improvement in their quality of living from the huge oil revenues.
3. Widespread corruption in the public and private sectors.
4. Violent gun crime.
5. An unmanageable 460 per cent increase in the population from five million to 28m between 1950 and 2020, due to widespread immigration from Latin American, Caribbean, and European countries.
6. An unrealistic foreign policy that did not enable the

government to successfully manoeuvre within the existing geo-political situation and trade relations in the Americas. Consequently, the country was unable to avoid destabilising interference during the Chavez Presidency when democratic, inclusive and equitable policies were implemented to meet the needs of all the people. It came from the US government, American corporations, and their local allies.

In the past

For many years, Venezuela had one of the highest GDP (Gross Domestic Product) growth rates in Latin America and the Caribbean, based on significant foreign direct investment in the oil, mining, services, and agricultural (rice and meat) sectors that produced a massive financial bonanza for US and European companies.

During the late 1970s and early 2000s when oil prices were very high, the governments of Presidents Perez and Chavez attempted to decrease the country's heavy dependence on oil revenues. They wanted to develop a diversified and sustainable economy with competitive businesses in the non-oil sectors. There were private investments in agricultural projects, cattle ranches, car assembly plants, hotels and eco-resorts, gold mines, and forestry projects. There were huge public investments in infrastructure - highways, hydro-electric projects, the electricity grid, airports, telecommunications, potable water, and massive public spending on social programmes, particularly in housing, health, and education. Yet, throughout its recent history, Venezuela has experienced major economic and social crises. How did this happen?

It was all about oil

First things first, Venezuela's dependence on oil revenues influenced the economic thinking of its public and private sector leaders, regardless of whether they were on the left, centre, or right of the political spectrum. Oil dependency thinking among the Venezuelan political, business, and labour leaders resulted in unrealistic expectations of what an oil industry could do for the development of a country.

They misunderstood, or choose to ignore, downplay, or deny the 'octopus-like' nature of the oil industry which has a mind of its own that is always working to ensure it dominates thinking on the development of any country. It is very smart and intelligent with considerable resources which enable it to recreate its dominance in new ways. It has many tools and tricks to protect and defend itself, and it camouflages its plans to resist any threats to its dominance.

Many times, with a 'friendly face', the industry has created in most oil-producing countries the oil 'Dutch Disease' of underdevelopment because the public and private sector leaders in those countries did not consistently prioritise their thinking on how to independently diversify their economies with an oil sector. Malaysia, which has had an oil industry for decades, is one of the few successful examples of the opposite.

Much of the Venezuelan public investment in infrastructural projects was wasteful with high cost overruns. Public spending on social programmes was unrealistically increased and that resulted in a significant growth of household consumption, and an increased demand for raw materials that local producers simply could not supply. Consequently, there was a continuous increase in all kinds of imports mainly from the USA, including food and goods that should have been produced in the country.

No comprehensive export strategy

There was no comprehensive export strategy. Most Venezuelan businesses were unable, on their own, to identify and successfully pursue export activities. There were no effective export promotion institutions which supported businesses to sustainably assemble and manufacture a diversity of value-added products and services for export markets. Why? The predominant thinking was 'Oil exports are relatively easy and that is what counts. We do not need to worry about all the challenges and problems when exporting other products and services'.

Disastrously, when oil prices declined in the 1980s and late 2000s, the oil revenues were not available to sustain large public investments in infrastructure and public spending in social programmes.

Consequently, Venezuela has one of the highest rates of violent crime in the world, increasing poverty, widespread corruption and jobs that are mainly in the public sector and the informal economy, rather than in the formal private economy.

No comprehensive economic strategy

The Venezuelan experience demonstrates that, without independent thinking, it is not easy to sustain economic diversification which requires continuously working to balance the development of both the non-oil and oil sectors, so that social programmes can be sustainably expanded over time.

What is Guyana doing to avoid oil dependency?

The Guyana government is on the right track. President Ali continuously talks about the risks and threats of oil dependency thinking. His focus is on raising productivity in all sectors through better management, mechanisation, and technology, and on structural and institutional reforms to take the country to the next level, rather than focusing exclusively on subsidies and tax concessions.

His government's comprehensive and forward-looking strategy is to implement pro-business and pro-poor economic policies that use the oil revenues to build modern infrastructure (roads, highways, bridges, and renewable energy) to support the development of a diversified, resilient, and competitive private sector economy in traditional, new, and emerging non-oil sectors, especially in agro-processing, ICT (information and communications technology), tourism, and environmental services.

To date, the PPP/C government is prudently managing public debt by sourcing development financing and servicing debt obligations at the lowest possible interest rates, and is ensuring that the debt-to-GDP ratio remains below 35 per cent, which is very low compared with the global average rate of 60 per cent. It is thinking and working on how to efficiently and effectively monitor, evaluate and adjust the capacity of the public and private sectors to annually absorb large public investments and public spending to avoid: debt distress and overheating of the economy, major projects with missed deadlines and significant cost overruns, high inflation and significant changes in the foreign exchange rate which could negatively affect the export opportunities for products and services from the non-oil economic sectors.

'One Guyana'

Through a 'One Guyana' strategy the government is working aggressively to overcome the political stalemate and to debunk ethnic fears and stereotypes. President Ali and his ministers are genuinely reaching out to Guyanese at the grassroots to address the concerns and needs in communities of all ancestries - Amerindian (Indigenous), African, Indian, Mixed, Portuguese, Chinese, and European.

Social programmes

Along with its political and economic strategies, the Guyana government is cautiously expanding progressive social programmes to meet the basic needs of every single Guyanese, so that no individual or family is left behind. In the hinterland communities, most Indigenous (Amerindian) Guyanese communities are experiencing economic, social, and cultural development. Across the country, there is modernisation of the education, health, sports, and recreational sectors. There is a massive house building drive with lower-interest mortgages, especially for low and middle-income citizens in all ten regions of the country. Consumption taxes on many products and services have been reduced or removed.

Child education grants were reintroduced. Increases have been made to the Old Age Pension as well as for persons on social assistance and those who are differently abled. Cash grants were given to farmers, fisher-folk, and retrenched sugar workers. Today, over 14,000 people, mainly women and young people, are employed in a part-time job programme in rural and hinterland regions. Over 17,000 Guyanese have been awarded free Guyana Online Academy of Learning (GOAL) scholarships to study at many reputable global universities. Funding has been increased for non-governmental organisations that are working to end domestic violence against women and children.

Minimising corruption and maximising international links

The government has commenced a programme to decrease corruption in key national institutions, based on UN (United Nations) and OAS (Organisation of American States) best practices.

President Ali is aggressively leading a realistic foreign policy that is expanding friendly political and trade relations with the USA, China, the UK, Europe, India, Ghana, Qatar and other countries. Guyana is playing a leading role in CARICOM (Caribbean Community and Common Market) activities to enhance food and energy security and to manage climate change.

But high GDP growth rates and the transformation of the economy will not automatically overcome the key social and cultural challenges that Venezuela failed to address: an upper middle class who tend to 'look out for itself' and who waste resources on lavish lifestyles and the consumption of foreign goods, high poverty, corruption, unmanageable immigration, and violent crimes.

Priorities for the next decade

Based on the thinking promoted by President Ali, here are some of my thoughts for implementation and/or strengthening over the next ten years, in order of priority.

1. Strengthen programmes to reduce violent crime and violence against women and children.
2. Expand 'One Guyana' economic, social and cultural programmes to foster socialisation and cooperation across all ethnic communities.
3. Implement a well-managed and targeted labour and

immigration policy, in partnership with businesses and labour organisations: to manage labour shortages and high unemployment in different regions of the country; to create more jobs in the private sector, rather than in the public sector and the informal sector; and to reverse the continuing 'brain drain' of Guyanese talent by promoting 'brain circulation' from the diaspora and by carefully managing the recruitment of skilled foreign employees.

4. Continue programmes to reduce corruption in the public and private sectors. Enforce them.
5. Transform public sector agencies and their systems into modern, non-partisan, accountable and transparent institutions, with the direct support and involvement of all communities and civil society organisations.
6. Continue to build a national consensus through regular public consultations and dialogue on the country's top investment priorities, and on the sequencing of major transformational projects.
7. Continue the diversification and modernisation of agriculture to reduce poverty in hinterland and rural communities.
8. Continue to ensure that foreign and local investments are not skewed towards the oil-related sectors by continuously increasing the percentage of the local private sector's contribution to Gross Domestic Product, especially in the agricultural, manufacturing, services (construction, housing, finance, insurance), tourism, and the Information and Technology sectors.
9. Because of Guyana's relatively small local market, create or strengthen export institutions to effectively support the private sector (micro, small, medium, and large businesses) to produce diversified exports for current and new markets.
10. Diversify the tax base by increasing the percentage of government revenues from the non-oil sectors, and continue to avoid significant fluctuations of foreign

exchange rates which could negatively affect the competitiveness of the non-oil economic sectors.

11. Continue to improve the public investment and public spending system.
12. Employ innovative approaches to encourage foreign and local investors to reinvest their earnings in the non-oil sectors, instead of exporting most of their profits.

In conclusion, it is a mistake to think, whether one is on the centre, right or left of the political spectrum or non-political, that a country which is dominated by oil revenues can transform its economic, political, social, and cultural sectors to the next level where all individuals, families, and ethnic communities can experience a higher quality of living.

leaders have to balance their thinking and actions on the development of both the non-oil and oil sectors. This will not be easy to do in Guyana, but President Ali and the PPP/C Cabinet are leading the way through independent thinking. I have listened to many of the speeches that he has delivered in Guyanese communities and at international forums. He mainly thinks, talks, and acts to develop a diversified, modern and resilient economy which is the essential foundation for implementing progressive and sustainable social programmes to improve the quality of living for all Guyanese. In today's world, Guyana is fortunate to have such leadership.

About the contributor

Geoffrey Da Silva is a former Minister of Tourism, Trade and Industry in the Government of Guyana from 1999 to 2001 and a former Chief Executive Officer of the Guyana Office for Investment from 2001 to 2011. He now lives in Canada.

Chapter Twenty-Two

Guyana and Kazakhstan: Lessons and an unlikely connection

Greg Quinn has served as a diplomat in both countries. He compares and contrasts those experiences

Guyana and Kazakhstan do not seem to have a natural connection but they both are (and will be) significant oil and gas producers, with troublesome neighbours and technical challenges in producing their oil. They also have similar issues to deal with in protecting the environment and ensuring indigenous groups benefit from oil wealth. There is potential for Guyana to learn lessons from how Kazakhstan has developed its oil industry.

At first glance there isn't much to compare Guyana and Kazakhstan. They are geographically about half a world apart. Guyana has a population of around 800,000 in a country the size of mainland UK. Kazakhstan has a population of over 19m in a country the size of Western Europe.

What they do have in common, however, are big neighbours who have been in the oil business on a significantly larger scale (and for a longer time) than they have. Neighbours who have not always been (or are) friendly. The highly technical nature of oil and gas production and the need to ensure the whole population benefits from oil are concerns of both countries.

Guyana is also developing fast. It is particularly (and rightly) eager to build its human capital and people skills. It wants to learn how to avoid the resource curse so many other countries have been affected by. It wants help in developing infrastructure and building what the people need, as well as in developing social and health services.

Kazakhstan has been though a similar journey and, despite

being in the oil industry for over 100 years, is still seeking to ensure its population benefits from oil and gas. This shows oil and gas is not an immediate fix to a particular problem and why it is so important to have a long-term strategic plan.

There may, therefore, be more similarities than you might initially think.

A brief history of oil in Guyana and the current state of play

When Guyana was a British colony there were small-scale oil finds on land. And whilst there was a suspicion there was oil offshore when exploration started in 1950 this was always considered commercially risky. Many big players came and went with no real results to show for their efforts.

It was only in 2015 (after seven years of exploration) that the ExxonMobil-led consortium made an initial find of around 300m barrels of oil equivalent. At that stage it became apparent that there were commercially viable (and significant) offshore fields. We thought those 300 million barrels were a lot. Little did we know. John Mair's 'A short history of oil in Guyana' (Chapter Two of this volume) provides a comprehensive timeline for oil in Guyana.

Eight years later, Guyana is producing 400,000 barrels of oil per day (bpd) with confirmed reserves of over 11bn barrels of oil equivalent. Production is expected to grow to 600,000 bpd in 2024 and 1.2m bpd by 2027 when the sixth offshore oil project (Whiptail) goes into operation. Meanwhile, it seems it is harder for the Exxon consortium (and other explorers) to drill a dry hole than a potentially commercial one. So far, around 37 wells have hit commercially viable oil. The number of 'dry' wells drilled is in (low) single figures! That's an astounding reality, in many ways unprecedented, and one of the reasons why the Guyana oil basin is so important and has had such an impact.

A brief history of oil in Kazakhstan and current state of play

Oil was first discovered in Kazakhstan in 1899 although production is deemed to have truly started in 1911 when the Dossor Field in Atyrau Oblast was developed by English businessmen.

Production plateaued in the 1960s and 1970s at around 500,000 bpd due to the highly technical challenge of developing deep, high-pressure reserves. This changed in the 1990s when the collapse of the Soviet Union led to Western international oil companies moving into Kazakhstan. Crude oil production was around 1.45m bpd in 2022. In comparison Canada produced 1.23m bpd; Iraq 4.28m bpd; Nigeria 1.27m bpd; Norway 1.69m bpd; the US 11.89m bpd; the UK 723,000 bpd, and Venezuela 730,000 bpd.

As a landlocked country, most of Kazakhstan's oil is shipped via pipelines or by rail and sea.

The technical challenges of developing Kazakh oil are shown by the Kashagan field in the Caspian Sea. The reserves are about 13,000ft below the seabed at a pressure of 770lbs psi and are high in corrosive (and dangerous) hydrogen sulphide. In addition, producing oil in a variable weather environment creates additional challenges.

How such challenges have been addressed means there is much to be gained from sharing experience between both countries. Kazakhstan has also had to deal with significant environmental issues (it was the testing ground for much of the Soviet Union's nuclear weapons and suffers the environmental consequences of that) and also needs to address issues around corporate social responsibility, including ensuring that all parts of society (including how Nomadic tribes, possibly comparable with Amerindians in Guyana) benefit from oil wealth.

Developing oil in the shadow of a noisy neighbour

Similarities also exist between Guyana and Kazakhstan in that they are (or have) developed oil in the face of a troublesome neighbour. In Guyana's case this is, of course, Venezuela. In Kazakhstan, a former part of the Soviet Union, that is Russia.

In many ways, you cannot compare Venezuela (with its unfounded claim on two-thirds of Guyanese territory) with Russia who have no similar claims on Kazakhstan. Indeed, relations between the two countries are cordial. But the reality is that Kazakhstan will have faced pressure in terms of having to transit oil and gas through Russia and having to listen to the views of Russia. They have walked a delicate line between Russia and the West. They therefore understand the problems of a troublesome neighbour determined to impose its views, no matter how unrealistic and unacceptable they may be.

Lessons for Guyana from Kazakhstan

There are other lessons to be learned. Kazakhstan's Sovereign Wealth Fund – Samruk Kazyna – is worth over US$70bn. It came into being in October 2008 and is focused on enhancing the competitiveness and sustainability of the national economy as well as preventing and addressing any negative impacts on economic growth of changes in world markets.

Samruk-Kazyna has historically played a leading role in easing the impact of global banking crises and other economic shocks and has helped reduce (if not avoid) how hard such shocks have hit the Kazakh economy.

As a Sovereign Wealth Fund, Samruk-Kazyna has therefore had some significant success. However, it has also faced challenges and has recently faced reorganisation following protests against falling domestic living standards and the need to address claims of corruption and nepotism.

All Sovereign Wealth Funds have their pros and cons. Considering a wide variety of such funds (and how they operate) from across the globe – including Kazakhstan – will provide a cross-sector panel of evidence which will help Guyana as it develops and models its Sovereign Wealth Fund, which they call the Natural Resources Fund. Currently it has $1,412,722,502 in the New York Federal Reserve Bank of New York. No one fund is perfect, and it would be wrong to rely on any one specific fund as a model.

Kazakhstan also implemented a strict local content law in December 2009 which put a high burden on oil and gas companies and on any contracts they may undertake. There was much grumbling about this law, but companies have knuckled down and worked with it. There are many benefits for the local populace. Guyana should consider the impact and implementation of this law as it, rightly, puts in place its own local content provisions. Any company will understand the importance of local content laws but at the same time they should be realistic and proportionate and, in certain circumstances where some jobs are highly technical, for example, to allow appropriate time for local skills to be developed.

Finally, a Kazakh Subsoil Oil Law also establishes the government's right to pre-empt any sale of oil and gas assets. This was used in 2013 when Kazakhstan pre-empted ConocoPhillips' sale of its 8.4 per cent stake in the Kasagan Field to India's Oil and Natural Gas Corporation. Kazakhstan ended up purchasing this stake (at no loss to ConocoPhillips) before selling it on to CNOOC (China National Oil Corporation). Whether, and when, Guyana should consider a similar law is open to debate.

There are potential lessons for Guyana from how a large country with a small population, with highly technical and complex reserves, ensures the country benefits from oil wealth.

A positive picture for Guyana

No one country has all the answers for Guyana. Many have something to contribute. I helped ensure links to Britain's Oil Dorado – Aberdeen in Scotland – when I was High Commissioner. These links continue to pay off and I encourage them to continue. Canada and others also have relevant experience. But Kazakhstan is in a unique position and one where there are similarities to Guyana. Learning from them has many potential upsides for Guyana.

Taking these lessons on board is vital to ensure oil and gas is the blessing Guyana so deserves and not the curse which has affected others. I remain whole-heartedly positive about the direction of travel in Guyana and have actively disagreed with many naysayers, but things cannot be taken for granted and effort is required. There can, and must, be no assumption of success. There needs to be constant effort, long-term thinking, and a strategic plan if success is to be guaranteed. That will take effort and commitment – on the part of the government, local business, international oil companies and support businesses, and civil society. It is incumbent on all those groups to work together to ensure that success.

Guyana has a once-in-many-lifetimes opportunity. It must not miss it.

About the contributor

Greg Quinn OBE served as British High Commissioner to Guyana from 2015 to 2020. In the course of more 28 years in the British Foreign Office he also spent 2012-2014 in Kazakhstan as Deputy Ambassador, and 2023 in Calgary Alberta as Honorary Consul.

Chapter Twenty-Three

Lessons from the Permian Basin, Texas

For the Permian Basin in Texas to prosper it needs a dedicated workforce which encompasses demands of its own that include an infrastructure of services to provide the lifestyle desired. So argues **Nick Vaccaro** in a chapter also published in *Oilman Magazine*

While the oil and gas industry remains cyclical in nature, many fail to plan and invest in the boom, knowing that the impending bust will rear its ugly head sometime in the future. With companies seeking to maximise profits by reducing costs, long-term future investment fades in importance. Instead, a 'get in and get out' strategy prevails but plagues the overall operation with worker shortages, limited infrastructure, and few plans for future investment. While enjoying mounting activity and high demand for product, the Permian Basin in Texas presently realises its limitations while meeting the increased demand.

The geopolitical stage has determined every facet of the global oil and gas industry and continues to do so. With various influential factors, like Russia's invasion of Ukraine and the LNG demand along the United States Gulf Coast, driving the market, the Permian finds itself in an interesting predicament. Its production continues to grow in conjunction with demand. That growth demands advances in technology and personnel, but limitations in crucial areas threaten not only the future of the play itself but the oil and gas market as well. If Permian production demands cannot be met, all will feel the outcome from shortages. Resolution can be waged through identifying those limitations and enacting a strategy to ensure success.

Establishing a local workforce

When scaling the Permian's workforce, it is no surprise that many of the men and women that make it up come from outside of the Midland-Odessa region. Other areas of Texas, and the states of Louisiana and Mississippi produce a significant portion of the workforce. With such a great demand levied on Permian production, the geographic area has yet to be able to staff the multiple job positions solely from locally. Instead, outside resources have continued to enter and assist.

Strategies have been implemented to cultivate a local workforce and they rely heavily on collaboration. Energy companies are being targeted to partner with local education institutions to offer specific courses needed to develop a robust pool of the next oil and gas workers. Knowing that the oil and gas industry demands unique and disciplined work ethics, steps are also under way to solicit US military veterans because of their proven discipline and pledge to get the job done, along with their ability to be trained and to display unrecognised talent.

An underlying issue still needs to be solved despite identifying multiple resources to create a pool of eligible talent. Leaders in the Permian have been faced with drawing that talent to the area and establishing a network of infrastructure that will fuel their desires to plant roots and commit to a long-term career with local residency. This surfaced early on as a challenge and has continued while improvement plans are implemented.

Developing a responsive healthcare system

The Permian undoubtedly offers an abundance of career opportunities. Individuals can migrate to the area and secure employment that provides growth in title, opportunity, and pay increases. Specific necessities, however, must be in place to attract these ambitious career seekers. While basic medical facilities exist in the Permian, it still needs more specialty healthcare facilities. The grim reality is having to drive great distances outside of the Midland-Odessa area should specialty care be required.

The Permian Strategic Partnership (PSP), an organised collaboration between federal, state, and local leaders, recognises the need for area improvements and works to implement solutions like establishing a robust healthcare system to help install and root a long-term local workforce. Programmes have received investment to meet the needs of patients, along with setting training initiatives specific to healthcare professionals. Within the past year alone, mental healthcare has received attention while minimising the costs incurred by Permian patients.

Primary medical care has been a challenging service to provide. The region has developed a mobile clinic model to deliver that. To staff these various healthcare positions, local colleges and universities have increased their scholarship and medical curricula to make Permian healthcare employment more attractive.

Offering essential services

History has consistently revealed that an oil boom brings a 'Wild West' mentality to basic living. While danger and excitement might find popularity in the cinema, it tends to deter the average employee. If career-seekers can achieve safety, the chances of moving their family and starting a new life in the Permian become more realistic. Basic infrastructure and services must be robust to catalyse one's desire to take a chance on the Permian and other shale booms.

Law enforcement and fire protection services needed improvement as the Permian activity increased; therefore, the need for betterment was identified, and action was taken. The quality and quantity of lifesaving equipment has significantly increased through donations, and funding has been secured to construct new and much-needed volunteer fire protection facilities throughout Midland alone.

With trucking playing a critical role in delivering the supply chain to and from the Permian, Tracee Bentley of the PSP identified a 4,000-driver shortage earlier in 2023, which directly influences safety and the need for capable medical response and services. Attempting to counteract the shortage, the trucking industry has lowered driver standards, resulting in an unwanted uptick in vehicular accidents. While legislation works to rectify these issues, agencies like the PSP have made strides in countermeasures, including contributions of emergency equipment, battery-powered jaws of life, fire extinguishers, and mobile landing zone kits for helicopters responding to emergencies. The quality offered, and the speed at which response occurs, have all seen improvements.

Advancing education

When discussing the education pillar of any adequate infrastructure system, it does not draw a singular focus on the university setting. While advancing colleges and universities and making them more attractive may lure students to the Permian area, consideration should be made for those adults already employed. Although they have surpassed their need for institutionalised learning, education still proves critical in the decision-making process.

Oil and gas workers with families look at the Permian with high expectations. Uprooting one's family proves difficult when making a career move, so the reward must be felt across multiple areas, including education. What the Permian offers the children of the workforce ranks just as importantly as it does to oil and gas professionals.

Now that the Permian activity has grown incredibly and fuelled the need for more workers, educational improvements are being made to improve the draw. Funding programmes have been instituted to improve the quality of education offered to children of all ages. These efforts, however, continue. While arguably late in response, the Permian is getting educational improvement not only at the student level but at the teacher level as well. Investments have been directed at teachers with National Board Certification programmes and Early Childhood and Teaching Excellence ones as well. Despite much effort, desire, and funding, it takes quality teachers to implement the programmes and make better education a reality.

Fulfilling future goals

115,000 new jobs will need to be filled by the year 2040, and this is not exclusive to just oil and gas. The harsh reality of the situation is that these are jobs directly associated with various areas of infrastructure, including emergency and medical services, education, utilities, and all others, representing their own cogs in the wheel.

The Bakken Formation, a rock unit spanning 200,000 square miles across North Dakota, Montana, Saskatchewan, and Manitoba is arguably one of the most prolific oil discoveries of American Shale. Its quick jump in activity without an adequate support structure mirrors the current state of affairs in the Permian. While the Bakken gained attention in 2006, proper planning fell short. Before its peak in 2012, an adequate support structure was never developed. Man-camps heavily populated the area during that time, providing basic living and dining accommodations for the incoming oil and gas workers. After 2012, however, towns like Williston, North Dakota, realised the need for a long-term commitment. Soon, man-camps were dismantled as permanent structures were constructed. New schools, additional restaurants, and lots of apartments and single-family housing have grown to accommodate a permanent workforce. Now the same process is beginning to unfold in Texas with the same needs identified to develop that long-term and local workforce.

The demand for gas thrust upon the Permian Basin has continued to grow and, as the United States faces a presidential election in 2024, the demand could even further increase. While the Permian Basin, like other shale plays, subscribes to 'no plan to fail', the effects of failing to plan are here and now. Provisions and accommodation must be implemented in the present to support the current demand and more than probable and sustained growth in the future.

A version of this piece appeared in *Oilman Magazine.*

About the contributor

Nick Vaccaro is a freelance writer and photographer. In addition to providing technical and copy writing services, he is an HSE consultant in the oil and gas industry with twelve years of experience. Vaccaro also contributes to *Oilman Magazine, Energies, American Oil and Gas Reporter*, and *Oil and Gas Investor Magazine*. He has a BA in photojournalism from Loyola University, and is based in the New Orleans, Louisiana area.

Chapter Twenty-Four

Lessons from Aberdeen, Scotland

Guyana and Scotland have strong historic links. Many of the early colonisers of Guyana were Scots and left behind towns and villages with Scottish names: Glasgow, Lethem, Tain, Inverness, and Alness. Those links have been renewed in the last decade in the era of oil. Here, former Lord Provost of Aberdeen **Barney Crockett** looks at what lessons can be learned today

A lot divides Aberdeen, Scotland from Guyana, South America. Aberdeen is on the northern edge of the cold North Sea rather than on the southern edge of the warm Caribbean.

Aberdeen has 50 years of experience of an oil and gas industry coming from the outside into the area and has moreover an industry focusing exclusively offshore. *The New York Times* described Aberdeen as the city 'with one foot on the seabed'. Guyana may have future as a nation with 'one foot on the seabed'.

Before oil, Aberdeen had a limited economy based on fishing and agriculture, much like Guyana, and has had to learn how to play host to companies from across the world. That will also be part of Guyana's future. Currently there are over 1,000 international companies working out of Aberdeen, including over 100 from nearby Norway.

Lesson one: Be open

A key lesson from Aberdeen is to be very open to the entry of international companies and not to put up too many barriers. Guyana should aim to be the most competitive place for international business in its region. It has a few in-built advantages which it must use to the utmost. It is the only country on the continent of South America to have English as its first language, it is part of the British Commonwealth, and has a respected regional legal structure. For companies to make long-term commitments the reliable rule of law is a crucial element. Because of this strength in Aberdeen, our legal companies now operate all over the world from Baku to the Falkland Islands.

Lesson two: Be international

An essential part of Aberdeen's economy is the internationalisation of such services. Guyana, with a strong educational history and the contacts provided by worldwide diasporas, can be well placed to benefit from this process.

Aberdeen was not unchallenged in becoming Europe's oil capital. Indeed, the UK government was keen that the nearest city to Aberdeen – Dundee – should take the lead.

It will be of interest to Guyanese which factors came in to play. Most importantly, oil companies suspected political turbulence in Dundee and this was a very strong negative. Whilst the harbour was superior in Dundee, those in control were less willing to discuss change and adaptability than the Harbour Board in Aberdeen. Dundee did not have an airport whilst Aberdeen did, though it was very small.

Lesson three: Good quality schools and quality public servants

These were the three main factors, though also mentioned to me were the quality of schools and the calibre of local public servants. All of these are factors which Guyana needs to consider.

At the time, when oil was beginning in Aberdeen, government pressure for speed was extreme because it was in the aftermath of the great oil shock and the UK economy was in serious difficulties. The source of the pressures on Guyana are different but the push is in the same direction. The key source of pressure is that the time for oil may be and (maybe should) be running out. Guyana should not be reliant on oil for many decades into the future but must try to capitalise on the years when there are still essential uses for oil whilst preparing for an energy transition for Guyana in step with the rest of the world.

Lesson four: Take down the barriers

One aspect of this is that Guyana must make all efforts to minimise barriers to development. This may mean accepting some delay in developing relevant local skills and meeting needs by importing workers. Aberdeen certainly had to do this. To offer one example, my first job in the oil industry was washing dishes on a diving barge. The other stewards were all from India while the rest of the crew were French and the divers British or French.

At the same time, international partners will have to be recruited to assist with relevant skills development in Guyana. Speed will be essential, even if local interests experience some displacement.

A local vs a national epicentre?

One dilemma which Aberdeen did not have was the relationship between the city and national government. The oil industry in Aberdeen is unique in that, since at least the late 1970s, national government has played a very small role.

Of course, this can never be an option for a country with a much smaller population and a much smaller economy. It is inevitable that the key oil developments will centre on the capital, Georgetown. And, given this inevitability, the government should make a virtue of it. Politically, this will pose challenges and will, for stability, require two preconditions.

In the first case, firm boundaries will be needed between the responsibilities of the national government and of the Georgetown municipality. The municipality will have to 'render unto Caesar what is Caesar's'. It will have to recognise the strategic role of central government.

On the other hand, the national government will have to build the capability of the municipality to ensure it can carry out efficiently the services required for an oil and gas centre. It will also have to co-operate in establishing a wider presence for the city in regional, international and world affairs. This has been essential for Aberdeen. Guyanese and Georgetown presence has to be maintained in venues like Houston for Offshore Technology Conference (OTC) and Ceraweek, and in Aberdeen for Offshore Europe, etc. Central government should seek to build a role for Guyana in relevant forums such as the World Energy Council, of which I am a member, but also for Georgetown establishing a relationship with the World Energy Cities partnership.

Problems?

In seizing opportunities in oil and gas, Guyana will be rightly anxious not to damage the brand it has worked hard to establish as the Cooperative Republic, holding in trust one of the world's most pristine natural environments – 83 per cent Rainforest. It is critical that Guyana proves to its own citizens and the wider world that this environment will be protected and that Guyana will play its full part in the coming energy transition.

Aberdeen, for its part, was perhaps the first of the main oil hubs to realise the need for such acceptance. Aberdeen City Council took an early lead for example in investment in hydrogen transport and has maintained this drive towards a hydrogen economy and is now working with BP on a project to use offshore wind power to produce hydrogen from water. Aberdeen also has the world prizewinning combined heat and power system, a regional waste processing service, including a new energy from waste plant to reduce carbon emissions, and an award-winning sustainable urban transport plan. In all of this, Aberdeen has succeeded in branding itself as a leader, not only in oil and gas, but also in energy transformation. That is something that Guyana should also make central to its development.

Companies like Orbis, Balmoral, and Apex Tubular from Aberdeen are already working in Guyana or providing products for use offshore in Guyana. In the early years, Aberdeen leaned heavily on the experience of others, particularly from Houston Texas. I hope Aberdeen companies may continue to contribute to the development of Guyana but I especially hope that public bodies from this area can work with Guyana to assist the development of relevant infrastructure and improved public services for its people

We are willing.

About the contributor

Barney Crockett was Lord Provost (Mayor) of Aberdeen from 2017-2022. He established links to Guyana in visiting the country in 2019. Aberdeen's University has since become a finishing school for Guyanese involved in oil – lawyers, technicians, and more. He remembers his first cricketing hero – Rohan Kanhai, the star Guyanese and West Indian batsman who played professional cricket in Aberdeen. Barney is currently an adviser to the World Energy Council.

Chapter Twenty-Five

Lessons from Ghana for Guyana: The good

Ghana in West Africa is a decade ahead of Guyana on the oil journey. Lawyer **Stanley Amarteifio** chairs the Ghana Chamber of Commerce Guyana (GCCG) in Georgetown and draws lessons - mainly good - from the former for the latter

The discovery of oil in Ghana marked a significant turning point in its economic landscape, ushering in a period of economic growth, leading to increased government revenue and foreign investment. This new-found wealth from Ghana's oil boom has been channelled into infrastructure development, education, and healthcare, improving the overall quality of life for many Ghanaians. Additionally, the oil industry has created jobs and stimulated various ancillary sectors, fostering economic diversification.

However, this surge in oil production has not come without challenges. Environmental concerns, such as oil spills and pollution, pose significant risks to Ghana's delicate ecosystems. The volatility of oil prices in the global market also exposes the country to economic instability. Furthermore, the 'resource curse' phenomenon, characterised by corruption, rent-seeking behaviour, and over-dependence on oil revenue, has the potential to hinder long-term sustainable development.

The Ghana journey

Ghana's journey in the oil and gas sector began with seepages of oil discovered in 1896, but it was not until 2007 that the further discovery of commercial quantities of oil and natural gas in the offshore Tano Basin paved the way for serious production in 2010. The first significant oil discovery in the Tano Basin was made at the Jubilee Field by a consortium of international oil companies.

Some commercial drilling of oil had started in the later part of the 19th century up until the Second World War in the western region of Ghana. Ghana primarily exported its crude oil to key markets including Europe, Asia, and the US. Ghana's recent discovery of oil has made the nation a magnet for Western oil companies such as the Irish company Tullow Oil, the American company Exxon Mobil, and the Norwegian company Aker Energy. The development of the petroleum industry has been key to reviving growth in Ghana's economy.

Ghana's venture into the oil and gas sector heralds both promise and peril. The upstream sector, dominated by international oil companies (IOCs) plays a pivotal role in this narrative.

The interests of the IOCs in Ghana's oil were advantageous as it created the need for the country to make certain legislative provisions as well as create certain bodies tasked with regulating and ensuring that the sector was properly regulated. These provisions included: the creation in 2011 of the Petroleum Commission, which oversees the issuance of licences to operate in the upstream sector as well as regulating the local content policies within that sector; the creation of the Petroleum (Local Content and Local Participation Regulations 2013 LI 2204 amongst others; the creation of the Ghana National Petroleum Corporation (GNPC) which acts as Ghana's national oil and gas company, with the mandate of exploring and exploiting Ghana's petroleum resources; and the creation of the Ghana National Gas Company (GNGC) which serves as the gas aggregator within the country.

Oil booms bring plenty trouble?

The sudden influx of expatriates led to the construction of apartment complexes, town houses, restaurants, and hotels which not only helped boost the economy but have also led to large infrastructure development giving a boost to the real estate sector and the circulation of wealth amongst the Ghanaian public. The surge in foreign direct investment and government revenue have brought evident advantages, but there are issues of transparency, mounting public debt, environmental degradation, and the failure of some of the IOCs to develop the oil-rich towns as mandated by the Ghanaian government.

The 'Dutch Disease' comes to Africa

Despite the potential for economic growth, Ghana has faced certain challenges such as the 'Dutch Disease', which is an economic phenomenon that occurs when a country experiences an appreciation of its currency and a decline in other sectors of the economy, often as a result of a sudden and substantial increase in revenue from the exploitation of natural resources, such as oil, gas, or minerals. The influx of revenue from natural resource exports, like oil, typically leads to a stronger domestic currency. This is because foreign buyers of the resource need to exchange their currency for the local currency to make purchases. As a result, the local currency appreciates in value relative to other currencies. This has resulted in a negative impact on non-resource exports: a stronger currency makes a country's non-resource exports, such as manufactured goods and agriculture products, more expensive for foreign buyers. As these goods become less competitive on the global market, the export-oriented industries suffer. This has led to a decline in production and job losses in these sectors. The appreciation of the currency has also affected export-oriented industries as well as adversely affecting local industries that compete with imported goods. The government of Ghana became heavily reliant on revenues generated from the oil boom and that may have led to resource dependency.

Oil and the environment

The oil boom in Ghana has also led to some forms of environmental degradation. The negative impact of oil in Ghana has included the destruction to biological and ecological resources in mining zones such as Ahanta West, Shama, Nzema East/West, Jomoro, Elembelle, among others. Environmental impact assessments have proven the extent to which the environment has been negatively affected by oil. Oil-related activities can result in water pollution. For example, the discharge of produced water (water that comes up with oil during extraction) can contain harmful chemicals and heavy metals. If not adequately treated and managed, this water can contaminate rivers and coastal areas. The development of onshore facilities may disrupt coastal ecosystems and natural habitats, having an impact on local biodiversity.

To mitigate these challenges, Ghana has implemented robust environmental protection policies. The Environmental Protection Agency, established in 1994, enforces stringent standards for pollution control and requires oil companies to conduct environmental impact assessments. Additionally, IOCs have to allocate funds for reclamation after decommissioning. Strengthening financial regulations and institutions is also vital to combat corruption and mismanagement of oil revenues.

Too many people, not enough infrastructure?

The sudden influx of people and capital into regions experiencing oil booms has also led to a strain on local infrastructure, leading to issues such as traffic congestion, housing shortages, and increased demand for public services. The oil industry requires extensive transportation facilities to move equipment, personnel, and goods to and from offshore drilling sites and onshore facilities. The increased traffic can put a strain on existing road networks, causing congestion, wear and tear on roads, and a need for additional road maintenance and expansion. This can divert resources and funding away from other pressing infrastructure needs.

Drawing lessons for Guyana

As Guyana embarks on its own oil journey, there are invaluable lessons to be gleaned from Ghana's experience. First and foremost, prioritising environmental protection and stringent regulation is paramount. Guyana needs to establish a robust regulatory framework to ensure responsible oil exploration and production, safeguarding its natural ecosystems and the livelihoods of its citizens.

Additionally, Guyana should prioritise transparency and accountability in managing oil revenue. Establishing strong financial oversight mechanisms and implementing effective anti-corruption measures are crucial to preventing resource mismanagement and ensuring that oil revenues are channelled towards sustainable development.

In areas such as local content, Ghana experienced IOCs partnering with Ghanaians who did not have the requisite skills, knowledge, and intention to operate in the sector. For a small fee, they were willing to be minority shareholders in the joint-venture companies operating in the sector to enable the IOCs to fulfil the requirements of them having a local partner. This was known as 'fronting' and is forbidden by Ghanaian law. The Petroleum Commission has successfully regulated the sector to ensure that IOCs do not engage in 'fronting'.

Guyana has the potential to face similar challenges and it will be prudent for the local Guyanese partners to participate in the oil operations in order for them to also build capacity.

Ghana' s oil boom embodies a complex interplay of benefits and challenges. While it has engendered economic growth, revenue generation, and job creation, it has also raised concerns about transparency, environmental impact, and economic stability. Striking a balance between harnessing the benefits and mitigating the risks necessitates concerted efforts from stakeholders is important. Drawing on Ghana's experience, Guyana can navigate its oil boom towards sustainable and inclusive development. Through responsible resource management and effective regulatory frameworks, both nations can chart a course towards a prosperous and sustainable future.

About the contributor

Stanley Amerteifio is a barrister and solicitor of the Supreme Court of Ghana, and CEO of the Ghana Chamber of Commerce Guyana.

Chapter Twenty-Six

Lessons from Ghana 2: The not-so-good

Guyana is trying to learn from other petro-states and their mistakes, among them Ghana in West Africa. **John Mair** takes a different look at the Ghanaian experience

Guyana Vice-president (and former President) Bharat Jagdeo, the de facto Guyana 'oil supremo', led a Guyana fact-finding delegation to Ghana in October 2021 to pick the brains of Ghanian key players. The traffic of expertise across the Middle Passage has been busy ever since. The President of Ghana, Nana Akufo-Addo, came to Georgetown in February 2022 to address the First International Energy conference. Many others have followed in his slipstream, including lawyers, tech experts and more. Branch offices have sprouted in Georgetown.

Does Ghana have anything to teach Guyana on oil? Well, the answer is both yes and no.

Good news

On the positive side, Ghana is a decade and more ahead. They discovered oil in 2007. Since then, they have benefited to the tune of $US1bn each year. Guyana has achieved that amount in 2022 and is only just at the beginning of their entrance to the field.

In 2019, Ghana was said to have the fastest-growing economy in the world. It was also praised for the steps it took to improve the regulation of the industry. Ghana was seen as a champion of growth for other nations within the continent and further afield to follow.

All was rosy...

Not-so-good news

But, and there are plenty of buts, Ghana is still plagued with the social problems of poverty, unemployment, illiteracy, drift to the cities, encroachment on the forests, and more. Oil wealth has not solved that.

Worst of all, they seem to be running out of money to pay their international debts. Ghana is in debt distress. In December 2002, their Ministry of Finance announced that they were unable to meet their obligations on international loans, whether Eurobonds, bilateral, of any other stripe. In their words: 'The combination of adverse external shocks (the Ukraine war, Covid, etc) has exposed Ghana to a surge in inflation, a large exchange rate depreciation, and stress on the financing of the budget. These factors taken together have put the sustainability of our debt at risk'.

In simple language, the piggy bank is empty.

From oil hero to oil zero

How did they get to this sorry state? Bad business. Political inter-party and intra-party interference in the oil industry has not always been good. When the party in power changes, oil companies exploit the vacuum.

The petroleum sector continues to be manipulated by politicians. This is done through the indiscriminate removal and appointment of technocrats and executives. The Ghana National Petroleum Corporation, the supposed regulator, has become notorious for being embroiled in several petroleum agreement scandals. Potentially, these are costing the Ghanaian taxpayer billions of dollars. There is still a lack of transparency and inadequate political will to propose and implement laws to the letter.

Recent revelations show that Ghana risks losing about US$1.5bn annually due to a 2020/21 gas supply agreement. The agreement has seen Ghana selling gas at a needlessly discounted rate of 77 per cent to a private entity. Ghana now has a surplus of gas.

The Petroleum Corporation had the mandate for petroleum exploration as well as imports of petroleum products for domestic consumption. Fiscal space was constrained at one time. Accordingly, one of the corporation's strategies was to use anticipated proceeds from future oil production from some fields to hedge oil price hikes. It also used proceeds from the sale of cocoa on the world market to directly pay for imported crude oil without having to look for foreign exchange to cover the cost.

These kinds of derivative transactions cost Ghana millions of dollars due to ill-informed advice from its financial advisers.

Contracts (production agreements) not sufficiently well enforced

In January 2023, the Africa Centre for Energy Policy (ACEP) produced an investigative report on Ghana which shows that it lost over US$882m on 14 petroleum contracts since regulators failed to be vigilant. In their findings, the investigative group described how the 16 contracts it examined were signed in the period between 2006 and 2019. These contracts included specific deliverables to ensure that companies did not merely hold on to the blocks but instead proceeded to exploration and production.

The production agreements (PAs) gave companies between six and seven years for exploration, with this timeframe divided into three stages. A company is supposed to meet the minimum requirement for one stage as a prerequisite before moving to the next phase. Failure to perform minimum obligations incurs a sanction in a form of payment to the state.

The ACEP report explained that the investment requirements for just 14 active PAs add up to a total of US$923m. Companies whose initial period has expired should have invested about US$750m in exploration. ACEP said the limited activity points to less than two per cent of the required minimum expenditure over the period, leaving Ghana losing out on over US$882m.

So, should Guyana send the Ghanaians back?

The legions of Ghanaian experts who have decamped to Georgetown may be bringing advice and experience but not all of it is positive. It is up to the Guyanese to sort the wheat from the chaff on that.

SECTION THREE: A LITTLE LIGHT HISTORY...OR AT LEAST 2019

John Mair

The history of oil in Guyana is very short. It is not yet a decade since first oil was struck, yet now oil gushes out of the Stabroek Block and maybe soon from other offshore areas.

It pays to look back at recent history. The first edition of *Oil Dorado* was published in 2019, riding the early crest of the oil zeitgeist. There have been changes aplenty since then. One Prime Minister, Nagamootoo, defenestrated; one petroleum adviser, Gossai, reaches the summit of influence and falls off; one Florida exile, Robert Persaud, returns to a senior Guyana Cabinet post.

This section looks back, briefly, at some of those contributions. It features some in political power, and some wanting and achieving it later.

The PM looks forward

First off, the Hon. Moses Nagamootoo, then PM and minister of information. He had wanted to be PPP president but left the party when passed over. Instead, he crossed the aisle. In 2019, he was optimistic:

'With the significant amount of money expected to flow to Guyana, the government has begun serious planning on how to utilise the expected oil resources to benefit all our people.

'Effective management of the oil and gas sector is crucial to its success. Towards this aim, an energy department has been established under the auspices of the ministry of the presidency, while a petroleum department hasbeen added to the ministry of natural resources. Upon the passage of a Petroleum Commission Bill, a broad-based commission will be established to regulate the oil and gas sector to ensure that the interests of the people ofGuyana are protected.'

Alas, none of these plans were to bear fruit. The people voted him and his government out of office in March 2020. It took five months for them to stop trying to dispute that result. After a period of attempted election rigging stopped by international pressure the new government of President Irfaan Ali took over. Nagamootoo is now in (permanent?) exile in Liliendaal, East Coast Demerara.

The former oil minister looks forward

Robert Persaud is the nearly man who has come again. He is the former minister of natural resources in Guyana. He lost office in March 2015 only just after awarding an oil franchise to some close colleagues. Exxon announced its first discovery in May 2015. Robert would also have liked to have been the PPP president. That was not to be. Instead, he came back from a 'sabbatical' in the US to resume office, this time as foreign secretary, when his party (finally) won the 2020 election. In 'Is Guyana ready for prime time?', written in 2019, he looked forward to the future rather than dwelling on the past: 'Oil will be ours to determine whether it will be a curse or cure,' he says, 'and I'm confident it will be one of the many cures to our decades-old social and economic setbacks. The work of attaining the elusive goal of national prosperity has now started with the beckoning of oil and gas!'

Robert Persaud's words

'Are we ready for oil prime time? Or more specifically, are we ready for an economy where the oil and gas sector can be the tallest pillar? And to answer the obvious question – what did we do to prepare for commercial oil production in Guyana?

'With limited resources there was only so much realistically that could have been done ahead of a commercial discovery curve. However, not lacking was the political will and national enthusiasm to get our nation in shape for this new, exciting bonanza sector.

'And so, with all that we have now confirmed, and with all the loud buzz and much hype about when the first barrel of oil is pumped up and piped into a tanker for refining, we are racing against time. So, putting our house in full order cannot be deferred nor delayed.

'Opportunities and threats abound as this new sector emerges to augment other traditional and existing social and economic activities to reshape the economic landscape of Guyana. Let's be cognisant that the road ahead can be slippery.'

Stirring words from the then King over the Water. Persaud came back from Florida and as Foreign Secretary is now charged with, inter alia, keeping the noisy neighbour of Venezuela from claiming the oil rich offshore territory and two-thirds of Guyana land as their own. This is a dispute which goes back close to one hundred and twenty five years.

The (now) government oil adviser looks forward

In 2019 Bobby Gossai was a Guyanese studying for a PhD at, inevitably, the University of Aberdeen (most of the oil experts in Guyana have been there). In 2023 he is the Senior Petroleum Coordinator, the government's chief adviser on petroleum. And then came a hiccup. It was announced in September 2023 that ExxonMobil had found a back passage to the Ministry of Natural Resources instead of dealing with the Guyana Revenue Authority. That individual was Bobby Gossai. He had negotiated, unseen, the Exxon historical costs to be put against profits down from US$214m to US$3m. The Guyanese taxpayer would lose US$105.5m. When this came out there was a furore and Gossai was disciplined, given a written warning, and having 15 days' pay deducted. It is not known if or when he will return to his old job. (By the by, he is the fifth oil adviser to the government of Guyana in less than a decade. Their shelf life is short.) Meanwhile Gossai returned to Aberdeen, on an 'overseas assignment' finishing off that PhD. Academia may be calling.

In 2019 he argued that a disciplined stewardship of the windfall from Guyana's new oil and gas finds could leadto great long-term prosperity. That means macro-economic action: 'One major imperative for Guyana is to focus on removing barriers to productivity across five key areas of the economy: the resources sector itself; resource rider sectors such as utilities and construction; manufacturing; local services such as retail trade and financial services; and agriculture.'

Bobby Gossai's words

'Whilst the best approach may vary somewhat, there are some valuable lessons from international experience to date that can be broadly applied. Guyana should consider the following if it wants to reap the full benefits of its resource endowments:

- Set expectations: To counter ill-informed pressure that could lead to wasteful spending, governments need to agree early in the process on the principles for how the resource wealth will be used and manage expectations among their citizens accordingly.
- Ensure spending is transparent and benefits are visible: Governments need to ensure that institutional mechanisms are put in place for a high level of transparency so that recipients see the benefits of invested resource windfalls.
- Smooth government expenditure: Setting a target for the non-commodity government budget balance can insulate public expenditures from volatility.
- Keep government lean: Resource-driven countries often suffer from bloated government bureaucracies. [...] One method to keep pay consistent is to benchmark wages to similar jobs in the private sector and to assign public sector roles a 'clean wage' without hidden perks or privileges.
- Shift from consumption to investment: Channelling some of the resource wealth into domestic investment and savings is crucial to start transforming natural resource wealth into long-term prosperity.'

Gossai was in Aberdeen on an 'overseas assignment'. Now he is back in Georgetown. He has returned to his job, not without much controversy. It would be interesting to compare his academic plan with Guyana's 2024 reality. But could it be that as the fifth Guyana government oil adviser to come and go in a decade he may no longer be in a position to bring his dreams to realisation.

The (unofficial) Guyanese oil historian looks at the perils

In a piece written in 2019 accountant and attorney Christopher Ram, who has chronicled in detail for years the historic search for oil in the local newspaper *Stabroek News*, argued that the clues were always there but it has taken decades of hope – and two border disputes – for oil to be finally realised.

Christopher Ram on Venezuela

'A quest that began in earnest some 170 years ago will soon become reality as Guyana – often the forgotten former British colony in South America – is set to become a top oil and gas producer on a per-capita basis in just one year. Between May 2015 and January 2019, ExxonMobil, the American oil giant, announced 12 'high-impact discoveries of oil and gas' with estimated gross recoverable resource of between four and five billion oil-equivalent barrels. (In 2020 that figure was up to 8bn; by 2023 it was up to 11bn.)

'The Venezuelan/British Mixed Boundary Commission examined it in a demarcation exercise in 1901-1905. Thereafter, the story became wrapped up in international intrigue, accusations of bribery and alleged collusion by the British and American governments to keep out a left-leaning government in British Guiana, before independence from Britain. That led to what is referred to as the Geneva Agreement of 1966 agreed between the UK and Venezuela to resolve the controversy over the frontier between Venezuela and British Guiana.

'Despite the agreement, Venezuela has remained steadfast in its claim, posing a great threat to Guyana's sovereignty and by extension its oil prospects. Following the announcement of the early recent discoveries, the energy and petroleum commission of the national assembly in Venezuela rejected the oil operations in the Essequibo region, claiming that it violated the Geneva agreement of 1966 and Article 10 its constitution. In 2015 the President of Venezuela issued a decree claiming the maritime area in which the oil exploration was being done, which he subsequently recalled.

'Legally, the fate of the controversy now rests with the International Court of Justice to which the matter has been taken by Guyana following the failure of a United Nations process, which saw the appointment of a good officer to resolve the controversy. Venezuela has refused to participate in the process. Practically, Guyana, it seems, is relying on the presence of a major American oil company in the controverted maritime territory to help protect its rights.'

(For more about this topic see Chapter Eleven in this edition of *Oil Dorado*: 'Oil and intimidation in the Guyana-Venezuela saga' by Ivelaw Lloyd Griffith.)

Christopher Ram on Suriname

'The border dispute between Guyana and Suriname had its genesis in the 18th century, when colonial powers (Great Britain and Netherlands) fought overland. In 1967, the government of Suriname stated that, in a treaty signed in 1799 between the Dutch and the British, all of the territory west of the Corentyne River was ceded to the colony of Berbice and the border was the left bank of the Corentyne from its mouth to its source. The Suriname government claimed that the Corentyne is a national river lying within its territory and not a boundary river.

'Guyana's position was that the south-eastern boundary between Guyana andSuriname was determined by international agreement among the governments of Brazil, Great Britain and the Netherlands in 1936.

'It took more than 150 years for a definitive resolution to permanently settle the correct maritime boundary between Berbice and Suriname. This was achieved in 2007 after Guyana had initiated proceedings for a judicial settlement under the United Nations Convention on the Law of the Sea, to which both countries were signatories.'

Suriname and Guyana are now at peace. Both have huge reserves of oil to exploit. Venezuela, though, is still very much the angry neighbour next door. As late as September 2023 they threatened to take back the disputed land and sea. This is an effective spoiler on oil companies applying for franchises in the disputed area. That aggressive act was condemned by the UN, Caricom, the OAS, and the United States. It did not deter President Maduro.

An analyst asks what's gone wrong with Venezuela and oil?

In an article originally published in *Forbes* in 2019 as well as in the first edition of *Oil Dorado*, Simon Flowers of Wood Mackenzie posed this question. Here are some the answers he provided at the time.

Simon Flowers on Venezuela (2019)

'Venezuela's slide from top of the heap to a virtual bit player in the world oil market is a slow-motion car crash. Production sank progressively from 2.6m. barrels per day (b/d) a decade ago, when it was third in Opec behind only Saudi Arabia and Iran, to 2m. b/d by Q3 2017. Decline since has been precipitous. Today it's just 1.1m b/d.

(By 2021 this was 650,000 bpd; by 2022 it was 760,000 bpd; and by 2023 it was 800,000 bpd.)

'The collapse of the economy has been one of the most severe (barring wars) since the fall of the Soviet Union. Six years ago, GDP per person was US$14,500, placing Venezuela just behind Chile as the wealthiest economy in South America and in the top 50 globally. In the past five years, the size of the economy has roughly halved. Besides severe recession, the country is grappling with hyper-inflation and a population exodus.

'A central factor in the shrivelling of the economy has been over-dependence on oil. Non-oil industries have all but vanished, their share of exports falling from around 25 per cent in the late 1990s to less than 3 per cent in recent years. The government borrowed heavily against rising oil revenues in the previous decade, fuelling social spending. When oil prices fell in 2014, Venezuela had minimal savings and no other buffer. The result has been a shortage of dollars to pay for imports of even basic goods, never mind repaying its international creditors or maintaining oil production. It's a window to a dystopian future for Guyana.'

What next?

So these were some thoughts from writers about the pre-history of Guyana's oil. They were all published five years ago in the first edition of *Oil Dorado*. Some of those thoughts were good, some bad, and some just plain ugly. But will Guyana learn from them? Only time will tell.

EPILOGUE

One should never forget that Guyana is much more than offshore oil. It is part of the Guyana Shield, the Amazon rainforest. Over 90 per cent of the land is covered with trees which, by and large, the country has succeeded in keeping relatively intact. Carbon credits, some from oil companies like Hess, have helped.

To wind down or to change gear at the end of this collection here's two of Guyana's greatest contemporary poets on the land that leads to the sea and the oilfield.

Rainforest Interlude (2019)

Grace Nichols

Nothing then, put to seek refuge
from the chaos of Stabroek Market Square
and the melting gold of the El Dorado-sun
and dive into the cool ambiance
of the Georgetown Museum – surfacing
among the glass cabinets of its stilled creation
drawn from the artistry of forest trees and rivers.
Like walking swimmers, we reacquaint with
Aripiama world's biggest fresh water fish,
Great Harpy-eagle, the startling, Hoatzin bird
and standing where my childhood left him,
old gold-seeking, gold-toothed, Pork-knocker,
saucepan and cutlass still hanging from his waist
still ready to cut his way through rainforest.

About the contributor

Born in Georgetown, Guyana, Grace Nichols is the author of many collections of poetry as well as one novel. She has received many honours for her work; they include the Commonwealth Poetry Prize (1983), the Guyana Poetry Prize (1996), and the Queen's Gold Medal for Poetry (2021).

The Sun Parrots are late this year (1992)

(For Chico Mendes, murdered Brazilian environmentalist)

Ian McDonald

The great forests of the world are burning down,
far away in Amazon they burn,
far beyond our eyes the trees are cut
and cleared and heaped and fired.
Ashes fill the rivers for miles and miles;
the rivers are stained with the blood of mighty trees.
Great rivers are brothers of great forests
and immense clouds shadowing the rose-lit waters
are cousins of this tribe of the earth-gods.
Under the ancient watch of the stars
all should be secure and beautiful forever,
dwarfing man, generation after generation after generation,
inspiring man, feeding him with dreams and strength.
But over there it is not so; man is giant
and the forest dwindles; it will soon be nothing -
scrubs spouting untidily in scorched black earth.
The sun will burn the earth, before now shadowed
for a hundred thousand years, dark and dripping,
hiding jeweled insects and thick-veined plants,
blue-black orchids with white hearts, red macaws,
the green lace of ferns, gold butterflies, opal snakes.
Everything shrivels and dust begins to blow;
it is as if acid was poured on the silken land.

It is far from here now, but it is coming nearer.
Those who love forests also are cut down.
This month, this year, we may not suffer;
the brutal way things are, it will come.
Already the cloud patterns are different each year,
the wind blows from new directions,
the rain comes earlier, beats down harder,
or it is dry when the pastures thirst.
In this dark, overarching Essequibo forest,

I walk near the shining river on the green paths
cool and green as melons laid in running streams.

I cannot imagine all the forests going down,
the great black hogs not snouting for the pulp of fruit,
all this beauty and power and shining life gone.
But in far, once emerald, Amazon the forest dies
by fire, fiercer than bright axes.
The roar of the wind in trees is sweet,
reassuring; the heavens stretch far and bright
above the loneliness of mist-shrouded forest trails,
and there is such a feel of softness in the evening air.
Can it be that all of this will go, leaving the clean-boned land?
I wonder if my children's children, come this way,
will see the great forest spread green and tall and far
as it spreads now far and green for me.
Is it my imagination that the days are furnace-hot,
the sun-parrots late or not come at all this year?

About the contributor

'Antiguan by ancestry, Trinidadian by birth, Guyanese by adoption, and West Indian by conviction', his own words, Ian McDonald is the de facto Poet Laureate of modern Guyana, a worthy successor to Martin Carter. Now 90, he has spent a lifetime producing an oeuvre of poems and novels including *The Humming-Bird Tree* (Heinemann, 1969; Macmillan, 2004) which was filmed by the BBC in 1992. He has been a Fellow of the Royal Society of Literature since 1970, been awarded a Guyana National Honour, the Golden Arrow of Achievement, in 1986, and awarded an honorary D.Litt. in recognition of his services to Caribbean sugar, sport, and literature by the University of the West Indies in 1997. His work can be found in *Ian McDonald's New and Collected Poems* (Peepal Tree Press, 2018).

Printed in Great Britain
by Amazon

45081064R00109